The Child He Gave Me, "SARA"

Obtaining Appropriate Education and Exposing Educational Myths, Disparity, and Inflexibility

Tamara Hise

With Contributions by Sara Hise

WESTBOW
PRESS®
A DIVISION OF THOMAS NELSON
& ZONDERVAN

Scripture taken from the King James Version of the Bible.

Scripture taken from the Holy Bible, NEW INTERNATIONAL VERSION®.
Copyright © 1973, 1978, 1984 by Biblica, Inc. All rights reserved worldwide.
Used by permission. NEW INTERNATIONAL VERSION® and NIV® are
registered trademarks of Biblica, Inc. Use of either trademark for the offering
of goods or services requires the prior written consent of Biblica US, Inc.

Scripture quotations taken from the Holy Bible, New Living Translation,
Copyright © 1996, 2004. Used by permission of Tyndale House
Publishers, Inc., Wheaton, Illinois 60189. All rights reserved.

Scripture quotations are from The Holy Bible, English Standard
Version® (ESV®), copyright © 2001 by Crossway, a publishing ministry
of Good News Publishers. Used by permission. All rights reserved.

Scripture quotations taken from the New American Standard Bible®,
Copyright © 1960, 1962, 1963, 1968, 1971, 1972, 1973, 1975, 1977, 1995
by The Lockman Foundation. Used by permission. (www.Lockman.org)

WestBow Press books may be ordered through booksellers or by contacting:

WestBow Press
A Division of Thomas Nelson & Zondervan
1663 Liberty Drive
Bloomington, IN 47403
www.westbowpress.com
1 (866) 928-1240

Because of the dynamic nature of the Internet, any web addresses or
links contained in this book may have changed since publication and
may no longer be valid. The views expressed in this work are solely those
of the author and do not necessarily reflect the views of the publisher,
and the publisher hereby disclaims any responsibility for them.

Any people depicted in stock imagery provided by Thinkstock are models,
and such images are being used for illustrative purposes only.
Certain stock imagery © Thinkstock.

ISBN: 978-1-5127-1006-9 (sc)
ISBN: 978-1-5127-1007-6 (hc)
ISBN: 978-1-5127-1005-2 (e)

Library of Congress Control Number: 2015914038

Print information available on the last page.

WestBow Press rev. date: 09/16/2015

Endorsements

In *The Child He Gave Me*, author Tammy Hise provides a narrative that is both informative and inspirational. Learning how to navigate an educational system that often expects adherence to a proscribed set of boundaries is a challenge when your child does not fit the defined mold. Educational advocacy requires a balance of diplomacy skills that are all too often met by negativity and suspicion. We walk with Tammy as she describes the path she blazes in order to insure the educational and socio-emotional needs of her daughter are met. Though her walk is fraught with challenges, Tammy's faith is an ever-present touchstone tempering each burden with His presence, thereby easing the load (Matthew 11:30 *MKJV*). Tammy's story is one of encouragement, hope, and obedience. As Jesus taught in Luke 12:48, "For to whomever much is given, of him much shall be required. And to whom men have committed much, of him they will ask more (*MKJV*).

Stephanie K. Ferguson, PhD
Director, Instructional Design and Academic Support, University of the Southwest, Hobbs, New Mexico
Former Director, Program for the Exceptionally Gifted, Mary Baldwin College, Staunton, Virginia

An amazing mom, a gifted child, and a remarkable, limit-testing journey that began with a question that should be at the forefront of every parent's mind: "If I don't advocate for my child, who will?" Whether they're gifted or not, better educational outcomes are possible for all of our children, and Tammy shows us how. *The Child He Gave Me* is a genre-blending look at what it's really like to parent when the system encounters an anomaly or, in this case, an exceptionally gifted child who transcends what is standard, normal, or expected.

Tom Ward
Director of Ministry Operations, Vision Nationals

Contents

To Sara

You are an amazingly courageous young woman! You are also one of the most sensitive and compassionate human beings I have ever known. Though you do not perceive yourself as truly inspirational, others do. I applaud you for the encouragement that this testimony of your journey will no doubt bring to other students like yourself. May you always pursue your passion for knowledge, accomplish all the dreams and desires of your heart, and never be without a good book in printed format! You have been blessed by God, and you are a blessing to others. You have always been a blessing to your parents, siblings, and extended family members. I pray you will continue to serve God and humanity by using your abilities in the ways God directs your life.

God sees not as man sees,
for man looks at the outward appearance,
but the LORD looks at the heart.
(1 Samuel 16:7b NASB)

Introduction

The public education system in America today faces many challenges, as do the students navigating its requirements and the parents whose children are pupils within it. Student achievements will continue to fall short in American public education as long as our system remains rigidly focused on age/grade-based instruction. It has taken more than a passive role to sustain the encouragement our youngsters required to successfully navigate and complete their public educations. It has taken our active involvement, fervent prayer, personal sacrifice, financial surrender, and commitment to love and nurture all the children God gave us—each a uniquely created individual. Admittedly, I lack qualifications in many areas, but without a doubt, my experiences raising five other human beings has given me qualifications to enter nearly every other career field that is known. Child raising has also exposed me to significant firsthand experience with our public school system. The years spent preparing young lives to enter our world as productive members of society have been the toughest, and the most revealing of my own limitations. Some situations that seemed at the time insurmountable or devastating have been only lessons in understanding that God has a specific plan for *every* individual life. Having been compressed by adversity and refined by both life and parenting experiences, I now see how the grace of God engulfed each of our family members when each least deserved it. The journey of raising our unique children has been chaotic. Some days I felt my life resembled high-velocity impact cratering. The lows have dropped me to my knees. Parenting has also been phenomenal, joyful, and treasured, with highs that lifted my eyes to the heavens. Our adult children are learning to adapt to their changed relationships with their siblings, and I am learning as a parent to embrace the adult men and women they have become (or are becoming). I never considered that God's plan for my life was to have been an advocate. I have never been professionally trained in "advocacy," yet it is clear *I am* a child advocate and an alternative-education advocate as well! By sharing my parenting testimony, the confines and constraints of our public educational system, and our experiences while advocating for the special educational needs of our child, I hope other parents and struggling students will be encouraged. All students should be encouraged to soar at their ability levels, to be confident in who God has created them to be, and to defy and conquer the obstacles that inhibit their advancing on their own education paths. To do so may mean taking an unusual, accelerated, homeschooled, or other alternate route.

ONE

Being an Advocate

Children come to parents through many avenues: fostering, blending families, adopting, and naturally. God is gracious to have been the original designer of adoption plans—accepting all His children equally as natural-born heirs! (Romans 8:15–17 NASB) When we married and blended our families, my husband and I knew there would be challenges. Our children were seventeen, seventeen, twelve, and seven years old at that time. Raising a child who has been entrusted to you and who cannot care for him- or herself, guiding a teenager (who should not be left to his or her immature reasoning), or continuing to love an adult child who has veered from the correct path is the most challenging career any human being can undertake. Without God's assurance, I would certainly have succumbed to the failings of my limited human understanding while attempting to parent young people with diverse individual traits. I believe that the blessing of becoming a parent is second only to that of the free gift of salvation. It is worthy of our utmost appreciation. I have not found anything that conveys the very sanctity of human life more astutely than the innocence of a child. Parenting successfully is not made easier in our modern world with its dangerous influences ("designer" street drugs,

1

rampant violence, prolific exposure to sex, and threatening political climate). In the best environments—homes, schools, and communities—there are no guarantees our children will become the men and women of our hopes and dreams. Often children of wonderful and attentive parents go astray, and many young people indulge in rebellious activities. In spite of the godly instructions given them by their parents, young people often choose to use their God-given free will in ways that seem good to them in the moment. When this occurred in our family, I initially perceived myself as having been remiss in my parenting. In truth, we are not human marionettes controlled by God in a show for His entertainment, and neither are the children He blesses us with. Our children have free will to make choices. Like us, some choices they have made in their lives and educations have not been the best choices. Also like us, their choices have confirmed parental restrictions and objections. Solomon said, "That which has been is that which will be, And that which has been done is that which will be done. So there is nothing new under the sun" (Ecclesiastes 1:9 NASB). All our children at one time or another, just like us, have been rebellious. I quickly discovered in our blended family that it was necessary to stretch out my love to heights and depths I had never imagined I would have to reach. Perhaps the difference between "good" parents and "successful" parents is the capacity to forgive and forbear. Accomplishing all that is required to raise compassionate, caring, human beings of integrity requires a lot of forgiving and forbearing on everyone's part. Stretching to meet the needs of the family as whole, and the individual needs of each child (who often cannot seem to decipher "needs" from "wants"), is a tough row to hoe in itself. Instilling a faith-centered core while doing it, which is the Christian parent's prime directive, is no easy task when confronting modern, secular morality. I required generous doses of forgiveness and forbearance while taking on the daily task of parenting our blessings. Parenting trials and tribulations come in a variety pack! My parental efforts did not always yield positive results.

Many times it was difficult to remember my children were blessings from God. I often thought parenting was a just another form of medieval torture, with the teen years being the most horrendous! It seemed as though there were always complaints from disgruntled youngsters who were convinced that they had been slighted by favoritism given to another (their perception). Words of wisdom I have repeated to myself over many years are "Fair is not necessarily equal—fair is when each child gets his or her needs met." Those words became my motto for parenting. One child's needs required more of our dollars while another child's needs required more of our time. Meeting each of our children's needs was the *fair* thing to do. Sometimes their perception of a need was skewed. Other times, their needs were beyond our own abilities to meet and sent us on the hunt for other resources. Some of our children needed more peer activities, some required an extra measure of emotional nurturing, one required more one-on-one homework assistance, and one youngster needed her own private stash of Girl Scout cookies to cope with the drama of the public high school years. One child needed EpiPen Auto-Injectors (epinephrine) for allergies; another needed albuterol inhalers for asthma; a third was accident prone (breaking bones multiple times, and hiding injuries); one son was repelled by all things "dirt" (wearing only crisp, clean, button-down shirts while pounding out concertos on the piano); and our eldest was routinely suffering from serious blistering sunburn but for whatever reason could not sacrifice the sixty seconds to have applied sun block! Our children have bungee-jumped off bridges, skydived, rafted rapids, ridden horses, and ridden in ambulances! Some have staunchly avoided gatherings, while others have run joyfully to them. They are introverts and extroverts. Each of our children has had his or her turn to be a high financial drain with specific needs or extracurricular interests to support. Each has had multiple turns with emotional, physical, and yes, educational challenges too! All of these areas were completely specific to each child, meaning, I often felt as though the endless carousel meeting various needs simultaneously was all I could do. How could I *impact* these impressionable lives?

All our children have at times acted like octopuses—agile, smart, and sneaky! Our adolescents often played both ends (custodial and noncustodial parents) against one another. What our children didn't understand was that their conniving brought costly returns to family court and ate up disposable income. Rare were any trips to amusement parks, annual vacations, bicycles, or cars for high school students. Normal sibling rivalry gave way to a united front against parent and stepparent (stretching the bonds of remarriage ever so shy of their breaking point). Normal stressors of family life were compounded by infection from disgruntled former spouses and well-intentioned advice from others. Some people, even our close friends and relatives, have criticized the ways we have chosen to meet our family's needs, the financial costs of our decisions, and the indebtedness we now carry as result. Even the size of our family has been fodder for those who are concerned about the "carbon footprint" on planet Earth (that our family is adding unfairly to—in their theory). Some we know were even betting on whether our blended family and new marriage would tumble into the abyss like our previous marriages. The consistently overwhelming challenge to meet the diverse needs of so many while attempting to "blend" into one nuclear family (and feeling scrutinized doing it) has certainly tested our marriage commitments to one another and the strength of our family's ties. The seemingly endless emotional upheaval made a harmonious homelife a fairy tale and certainly not our reality! In fact, the endless responsibilities were like the tentacles of an octopus gripping its prey. All our lives were entirely too stressful (though probably more normal or typical in our modern American society than anyone wants to admit). There are many parents in situations just like ours who are living with these same challenges today.

I was keenly aware I lacked the wisdom of Solomon, was absent the prayer life of the Psalmist, and did not cultivate the quality traits of the woman in Proverbs 31! I knew my faith more resembled that granule of a mustard seed we've all heard about. I wasn't a believer that my tiny faith was sufficient. Certainly I was not convinced that "Nothing would be impossible for me" (Matthew 17:20 NASB). The daily, sometimes hourly, demands often felt impossible to juggle. My idea of accomplishing great things was limited to collecting our younger children from their Christian afterschool program on time (avoiding the $5.00 per minute late fee). It was "great" if I could actually work a full five-day week (because no child was home ill). Greater still was avoiding a traffic accident on California's Interstate 5 during rush hour. Preparing a thirty-minute dinner? That was bonus greatness! I couldn't imagine that great, "godly" things could possibly come from *my* house in its chaos and disarray. Hadn't God looked down on our apartment on the third floor of a huge complex in the city where our teenage boys were sneaking out at night to throw my vegetables from the rooftop into the traffic lanes below? Wasn't I doing a fabulous job parenting? I had faith only the size of a mustard seed, and I definitely required my own stash of Girl Scout cookies to cope. Like many of you reading this book, we were average, ordinary, working-class parents trying to raise up responsible young people. Greatness would have to come from God's influence and the Holy Spirit's active nudging of our offspring to become the men and women God created them to be. Those days, I thought I lacked the faith that He could use me to accomplish anything more than a nice family-size casserole. There is no doubt both my husband and I made many mistakes during the child-raising years.

Our children once were first in line to testify of our parental failings, but now as adults, they recognize some merit in our decisions. These days, it is also abundantly clear that God has in fact done great things within my seemingly small faith. He has continually accomplished His goals for the children He gave me. If I have helped to raise up men and women who can accomplish beneficial things for our society and our world while pursuing their individual godly purposes with passion, I am confident God will not care about the level of debt we currently have, formerly had, or in the future might place on these earthly books. Likewise, I do not think God is concerned about the increase to the size of any theorized carbon footprint caused by the children He gave me. This doesn't mean I embrace irresponsible financial freedom or bad stewardship of environmental resources; it means I believe God's children are the most important priority to Him—not our personal earthly income, assets, debts, or liabilities. In our current global economy, where my own nation is $18 trillion in debt, I think God is aware of greater math, tax collection, and stewardship issues than those of our repeated (and interest-bearing) Parent PLUS student loans. My parenting decisions have had both wins and losses, but in thirty-three years, God *has* moved my focus off the size of my faith and onto His faithfulness!

Becoming a first-time parent sounds so romantic and exciting (especially to the young and well-rested couple). Babies are delightful. Who can resist pulling an infant's sock off *accidentally* (on purpose) to reveal such tiny and perfect little feet. Parents enjoy viewing their child's intricate tiny fingers and the perfection of each delicate eyelash. Babies coo softly and smile sweetly, and when they sleep, *most* do so peacefully. Fretting over the fragile tiny beings that have been entrusted to parents should become the new "normal" focus of all parent's lives. We should all be amazed at the wonder of their creation! Experienced parents also fret over and focus on their youngsters, although the initial romantic idea of the parenting experience has usually given way to the reality of the workload. All our babies too quickly develop into legal commodities known as "students," and most take their assigned seat in our public education system. The education system stressors that all parents deal with come quickly—like a runaway train! In every state of our nation, for twelve compulsory years per child, students and parents alike must endure the daily and weekend homework assignments. Many also participate in sports program requirements, band practices, and reading, math, and spelling competitions. Parents (involved, active, able parents) drive, go, pay, support, cheer, sew uniforms, transport instruments, and check homework. They get their children to school on time, and with education budget cuts nationwide, parents also volunteer as coaches, room parents, and paper-graders for their children's teachers. Going to school has become a marathon of activities, deadlines, and requirements that are exhausting on both parents and students. Whatever you do, parents, "do not be late for pickup time!" We often felt inadequate in meeting the requirements for children in multiple grades and schools, but like most parents (who find energy they did not think they had), we did our best to attend events, bake cookies, support fundraisers, and sit in the band section while cheering at high school football games. We chaperoned on school buses and supported science-fair projects and displays. We hosted field trips to our small farm (there's nothing like fifty six-year-olds enthralled by a petting zoo). I read "The Three Little Pigs" in kindergarten class (with a live piglet for five-year-olds to enjoy), and I even took the live ugly duckling to third grade!

Sadly, American society appears to have lost respect for the contributions of parents. While some parents are not deserving of merit, the majority of American parents *are* loving and nurturing, and they are involved with their children. Parenting should really be rebranded to more adequately reflect its major job duty: *advocating*. Parenting requires significant advocating! Our public schools today reflect a growing number of parents failing to advocate for proper behavior, manners, and respect for authority. However, most parents still continue to instruct children in these basic societal morals. They also advocate for opportunities that will teach their children to be charitable and to form good work ethics, and they advocate for their children to be involved in community service projects. Activities such as scouting, civic-club participation, and church youth groups are well attended by children *and* their volunteer advocates. These children have advocates who believe involvement in community assists in developing worthy traits. Some children are fortunate to have stay-at-home advocates, while some advocates must work or chose to work in career fields outside the home. Advocates balancing both family and career are common in American society. Having a career outside the home, achieving financial security, rising in one's employment status, or possessing political clout continue to grow as achievements viewed as highly esteemed. Being a stay-at-home parent generally remains thought of as a lackluster position. It is sad to say that while American society has promoted ideas of equality and embracing diversity, it has not exhausted the mindset that being a stay-at-home advocate is a less challenging and less esteemed achievement. Full-time child advocacy is largely viewed as a lowly task for the underachiever who obviously did not go to advanced levels of education or who lacks motivation to work a "real job." This is of course an untruth endured by many a stay-at-home parent. Raising children is not a *less* satisfying or a *less* important work than that of a professional career outside the home—it is a physically and mentally exhausting undertaking to produce unique and spectacular results! It is a choice that parents make that earns them no paid vacations, sick leave, or future retirement income. It is also a career position that too often finds these parents degraded by income earners.

I voluntarily left my very well-paying professional career in Los Angeles County, California. I gave up my private office. Perhaps more eye raising was surrendering my very esteemed reserved parking space in the city—the space with my name on it! I tossed my embossed-name business cards in the garbage and moved to an older-model manufactured home in the rural desert—to raise our children! I have had good and bad work days in my stay-at-home advocacy profession—it has definitely been a *real* job! When it came to my motivation level, I chose to advocate for the children God gave me. Family is important, grandparents *do* age, the young are impressionable, and seeking after greater amounts of money too often blinds us to more important priorities. I wanted my children to be strongly influenced by my morality and not to spend the majority of their consciousness influenced by the values of others who cared for them (while I sought after the riches of this world). Financially, it has been constantly difficult to support our family on a single income, even after relocating to a lower cost of living area. I believe that God values investing in relationships more than investing hours, days, and years striving for material and monetary gains.

Certainly my career income (offset by expenses of high-cost Los Angeles housing, child care, and after-school program costs) did not provide the quality of life in the city that living in the rural desert has allowed us. I am proud to have been a child advocate who has worked from our home. And yes, I too *am* a feminist, believing women should have opportunities and options to pursue the purpose and develop the attributes God gave to them. I also believe that both choices (to pursue a career outside the home and the child advocate working at home) should be equally valued for their contributions to society. The stay-at-home advocate preparing the next generation for impacting our nation and our world is usually highly motivated. Influenced by their advocates, the children being raised today may make exciting discoveries in science, space exploration, or medicine or improve foreign policies and bring stronger ethics to politics. Some may choose to work with charities for the good of humanity or to support and defend their nation. They may become great musicians or artists who were encouraged to pursue their passions through artistic expression. No doubt some will become advocates themselves! Some may answer their calling in service to the Lord, Jesus Christ! The stay-at-home parent has a huge influence on the future of their nation and our world, and with that opportunity comes a huge responsibility that should not be viewed as less significant than the contributions of the workforce salary earner.

Our own children and our marriage may have been more strongly bonded because (keeping the bar high and stress levels at maximum) God added to our family chain a final link that connected each of us in a special way. This was one of several reasons for our decision to leave the city. It also placed my husband and me in that category known as "late-in-life parents." I did not think myself *old* until the medical profession diagnosed my aging reproductive issues for me— as I was approaching age forty. During the years since the arrival of our youngest, I have sometimes thought back to a visit to my obstetrician and found comfort in my husband's faith. My husband and I were informed of my high risk factors for fetal abnormalities such as Down Syndrome. We listened to research statistics, the list of possible defects, and my own age-related health factors. We were advised to undergo in utero tests (with normal risks of miscarriage). These tests would determine if our little fetus was going to be "normal." My husband then calmly responded, "Why? We're going to love it no matter what we get." There was never a question of our commitment to advocate for whatever "special needs" we might encounter. We had been made acutely aware that the future might require us to kick open new and different doors of opportunity. Those doors would likely be some we had not encountered with any of our other children. During those uncertain months of pregnancy, my advanced maternal age had been commented on so often I was inspired to name our daughter in honor of the Biblical *older* mother, Sarah. With two of our children already adults, we certainly were not novice parents when Sara was born. We had survived normal ages and stages of child development four times and with both sexes. In spite of our experiences, we appeared to suffer from greater fear and concern over our cherished midlife blessing than we had when our older children had been much smaller. Perhaps our understanding of society's changing moral values, the increase in random acts of violence, or our enhanced appreciation for the miracle of childbirth moved us to greater fear and concern. Or it could have been we knew our youngest would someday be a teenager like her siblings, so we cherished her early stages of her childhood development. The addition of Sara drew our family closer together, and each child bonded with their significantly younger sibling. She is a special link that connects all her siblings in her blended family, and each has an undeniably different relationship with her.

Mistakenly, I thought parenting challenges would be easier after my eighteen prior years on the job. They have not been. We knew all the children in our home were uniquely created and that each child was equipped with individual Biblical "gifts" as well as individual needs. They are musically gifted, faithful, compassionate, driven to bring political justice, and outspoken for those without a voice. They are intelligent thinkers, hardworking laborers, creative artists, and curious explorers. Some have occasionally been lost in their own search for self-discovery. They have lost their way, lost at love, lost their jobs, and sometimes questioned the good fortune that has come upon others while they have struggled. They have questioned their world and sought their God. They are remarkable human beings! Each of our children received his or her own talents and abilities, and I am delighted that they are using them in a variety of activities and service. I hope each will continue to pursue his or her individual accomplishments with the unique gifts God gave him or her. I pray for each to receive stronger faith in God's provisions to tackle his or her life challenges. I hope they all experience fulfillment by their choices and follow the direction God leads their lives. I am immensely proud to be their mom (although like all mothers I have had difficult days with decisions they have made). At various times, each of Sara's siblings felt she received significantly more attention for her unique God-given gift. Joseph's brothers were not pleased about their father's doting on him, and they didn't appreciate Joseph's God-given gift of interpreting dreams either! (Genesis 37:19 NASB) Our adult children now understand that God gives everyone something unique and special to share with others and a potential for effecting change for a better world. "There are different kinds of gifts, but the same Spirit distributes them. There are different kinds of service, but the same Lord. There are different kinds of working, but in all of them and in everyone it is the same God at work" (1Corinthians 12:4–6 NIV). Children grow up in time, and all her adult siblings are now proud Sara is developing her gifts just as they have developed their own. Sara was uniquely created and we had quickly noticed she was indeed providing us some challenges we had never encountered with any of our other children, combined or individually. The chart of pediatric milestones and Sara were always off-kilter. It had never occurred to us that Sara's special needs would be those of an exceptionally gifted mind.

We realize that Sara's gifting is certainly rare and beautiful; however, it is not the sum and total of her being. It is only a small part of the beautiful person Sara is, but that "gifted" part has required me to stretch in ways I never considered, to dedicate hours I did not think I could find, and to fight battles with armor I had never worn. As their mom, I knew each child's specific interests and abilities and advocated different doors of opportunity for each. Not always did our children think doors of opportunity *should* be kicked ajar and them pushed through the opening! When it came to Sara, doors of opportunity were fewer. All were bolted more securely, and Sara was too long delayed by legalities. She needed a ruthless advocate (and maybe the assistance of just one of God's angels) to stand up for her right to use and develop her God-given gift. Sara happens to have a God-given and profound desire to learn as well as a remarkable ability to process learning opportunities presented to her. When others discovered the performance levels in education Sara has achieved in half or less the "normal" timeframe, they have exclaimed, "She's a genius!" or "She's a prodigy." I don't think of Sara as a "genius." I think of her as our child. Some have commented, "That's such a blessing." Undeniably so! Each of my children has been a blessing to me. "And now it has pleased You to bless the house of Your servant, that it may continue forever before you; for You, Oh Lord, have blessed, and it is blessed forever" (1 Chronicles 17:27 NASB). I will never be as wise as Solomon, never be the prayer warrior of the Psalmist, and most certainly never attain that Proverbs 31–woman status, but I have put on the full armor of God and fought battles for *all* the children He gave me. Frequently, it has been necessary to remind myself, "If God is for us, who is against us?" (Romans 8:31 NASB)

The challenge of keeping up with a youngster whose mind soars ahead at rates of speed faster than my own, who drives me to dictionary lookups, and whose ability to comprehend complexities far more advanced than my ability levels has at times tested my confidence, stretched my competence, wearied my patience, and defined my resolve. The path through education has been fraught with skeptical teachers, administrators who cannot break from policies, and school districts with fears of liabilities. School registration forms require and teachers request information about their students. Understandably, they want to place pupils in the best classroom situations for their success. Yet, full disclosure also leads to scrutiny and prejudice. I cannot begin to count the number of times I've had to disclose Sara's level of competency only to have others look at me as though I had grossly exaggerated. These educational "experts" often looked at me as if I were wearing underwear on my head. Over the years, incongruent remarks to facial expressions were common from educational administrators, teachers, school counselors, other mothers, and even close friends and family. Verbal responses often said, "That is wonderful!" while body language said, "You're one of those mothers pushing your child forward to succeed at any cost." No, I was not. I was chosen by God to raise a toddler who assembled puzzle pieces upside down because she didn't like the picture. I was appointed by God to expose His child to the wonders of His world and to the excitement of discovery. I was tasked by God to maintain pace with an educational marathon runner whose desire was to absorb every subject in academics! I am proud. Not because Sara has reached educational goals sooner than others, but because she has done her best with what God has given her. I am also proud God chose *us* to parent another wonderful addition to our family. Although, admittedly I have often found myself asking why God thought I would be competent in this position. There will always be those who roll their eyes and cringe with facial expressions conveying, "Every parent thinks his or her child is a bright and shining star." The truth is, yes, I do! Every parent should think this way. Every child is a bright and shining star! Every child should be able to achieve his or her personal best in an educational environment that is both willing and able to provide the challenge levels each pupil requires. Unfortunately, my opinion of our current public educational system is that it is simply no longer designed to provide this type of individual-student focus. Simply put, I believe we have governed learning out of education. During our journey to secure the appropriate education for our daughter, I have been like sandpaper that has rubbed against the grain of many educators. Some have applauded our courage to pursue unconventional routes. Others respected Sara's determination to obtain higher challenges for herself. While setting precedents within our K–12 school district and our county community college district, Sara's educational path has unnerved most in the education profession. Perhaps some were and are too content with the educational status quo. Likewise, I am sure there were those who were genuinely concerned about Sara and truly feared she would one day regret her accelerated path through education. As her parents, we saw the emotional expense of the slower traditional path as most detrimental to Sara. Mr. Andrew Solomon, a lecturer in psychiatry at Cornell University, wrote an essay for the *New York Times* in which he stated,

> While it is true that some parents push their kids too hard and give them breakdowns, others fail to

support a child's passion for his own gift and deprive him of the only life that he would have enjoyed. You can err in either direction. Given that there is no consensus about how to raise ordinary children, it is not surprising that there is none about how to raise remarkable children. Like parents of children who are severely challenged, parents of exceptionally talented children are custodians of young people beyond their comprehension. (Solomon, "Would You Wish This On Your Child?", 38)

Wonderfully stated! *I* am the "custodian" of *my* child. In the absence of a consensus on how to raise our remarkable child who has been entrusted to us by God, my husband and I have chosen to support Sara's passion for learning no matter how unfamiliar or unpopular our educational decisions on her behalf. This does not mean as parents we forged ahead blindly into the unknown. Rather it indicates our parental responsibility was to seek what was the best opportunity for the most *appropriate* learning experiences for the child we have been blessed with.

To have been our child's advocate was good—to have been a responsible and informed advocate was best! Becoming an informed mother and an effective advocate has taken more research time than I ever imagined. It has also taken a strong conviction to rebuke the naysayers and withstand the tremendous negativity. Today, our home is nearly an empty nest where my husband and I have received our American Association of Retired Persons (AARP) invitations but are still parenting a teenager. These days, there are still challenging situations that sometimes cause me to feel parental self-doubt (but only momentarily). As I have grown older, it is refreshing and (dare I say it) satisfying to acknowledge that I have been only a custodian of the children God entrusted to us for a season. They are His, and each has his or her God-given purpose to pursue in his or her own lifetimes. My job was and is to advocate for each of my children until he or she is able to advocate for himself or herself and navigate our world on his or her own. I have learned that God-given gifts (a propensity for achievement, understanding, or contribution in any area) that cannot be developed are very much like needs that cannot be met. Unmet needs and gifts that are arrested in development can both result in great frustration and depression (as our experience parenting has taught). As their mother, it was my job to ensure that they had open access to opportunities for developing their God-given potential and accomplishing His purpose for their lives. While advocating for Sara's right to her "appropriate-education" opportunity, I have learned just how much I have walked by faith—and not alone. It has become apparent that "We have all benefited from the rich blessings he brought to us – one gracious blessing after another" (John 1:16 NLT).

Advocating for the children God gave me to best provide what they needed (not what they thought they wanted) has been by far the more difficult of my career fields. Yet it has been the work our society has devalued. I noticed that when others asked, "Where do you work?" if my response was "I'm home with our children," then I was *just* a stay-at-home mom! But if I said, "I'm a child advocate," suddenly I was interesting, worthy of conversing with, treated as though I had a few brain cells. Perhaps I had something to discuss or an interesting life! The only thing that had changed was the rebranding of my job title to "advocate"—which of course is what all parents are supposed to be! I believe the thirty-three years I have spent in my advocacy career have prepared great minds and healthy bodies to impact the Kingdom of God for the Lord, Jesus Christ. I also believe every child's advocate is participating in the single, most important career field on planet Earth.

T W O

Meet Lucy!

As we delivered Sara to her first day at her assigned public school, we had hopes that our daughter would have a positive introduction to school experience, make lasting childhood friendships, and love being in her learning environment. From the beginning the parent/teacher conferences were not very positive. Sara apparently couldn't jump rope. This didn't surprise me since we lived on acreage in the desert and I had never given Sara a jump rope. What mother gives her child instruments to kick up the dust levels from desert sand? Sara also couldn't pump her legs hard enough to start herself swinging on the swing set. I am not certain how many trips to the park her father had taken her on, but I'm sure he always pushed her on the swings! Apparently Sara's athletic skills at hopscotch were lacking, and anything involving a bouncing ball was apparently challenging for her. The teacher was very concerned about the need for Sara to have "good physical balance" at her four years and eleven months of age. Sara's kindergarten teacher was also very concerned that Sara often displayed a heightened startle reflex and cried at loud, unexpected noises. Initially, I shrugged these comments off and attributed Sara's perceived shortcomings to the benefits of a rural country atmosphere. Being surrounded by farm animals, it would not be surprising for a very young five-year-old raised in a quiet farm setting to be startled by loud and unexpected rumblings. Unless you raise turkeys or guinea hens, or perhaps it is feeding time for sheep, livestock doesn't make much noise. As God's timing had dictated, Sara's siblings were either adults or quickly approaching adulthood, and they were rarely home to create sudden, unexpected, loud noises. Still, it did appear that Sara was always on the kindergarten teacher's list for something! She resisted the teacher's instruction to use a fat crayon when she preferred regular crayons. Is it not the goal for children to transition to a normal-sized writing instrument? Sara was punished for not obeying the traffic rules on the tricycle roadway. After being punished, it was determined Sara had been a victim of "mistaken identity." Sara was stanchly opposed to others touching her, she did not like strangers to talk to her, and she clearly understood her personal space boundaries. These were not viewed as positive "socialization" traits. Repeated teacher conferences and assessments reflected "Sara's need for socialization skills."

Socialization skills were consistently brought up for discussions. At one point, the kindergarten teacher went as far as to actually state to me that she believed "Sara may be autistic." This statement infuriated me. Actually, it led me to seethe in anger while wondering if teaching credentials now also came with the qualifications to diagnose autism spectrum disorders! God's instruction to "Let all bitterness and wrath and anger and clamor and slander be put away from you, along with all malice" was an ongoing process for me during Sara's kindergarten year (Ephesians 4:31 NASB). My most vivid memories, which should have been my daughter's joyful introduction to a formal learning environment, are Sara expressing on many mornings, "Can't I just stay home?"

I was not aware that balance issues such as the inability to jump in place or stand on one leg more than two seconds were characteristic of autism. I was unaware the teacher was evaluating Sara's startled reactions to fire drills and other loud unexpected occurrences in comparison to autism characteristics. Sara's kindergarten instructor had indeed been seeing something "different" in Sara. It was not however an autism spectrum disorder. Autistic individuals are often interested in facts as are gifted individuals. At times, both autistic and gifted individuals might have difficulties in social situations. Some traits indicative of highly gifted children are displayed by gifted students who do not have "true" peers. For a better understanding of this "overlap," the table below shows a few common traits shared by both special-needs groups. It explains why educators might be confused by characteristics they see pupils exhibit within their classrooms.

Table 1—Brief Comparison of Traits

Autism Society	National Association for Gifted Children
Doesn't play a variety of games and activities	Intensely focused on passions—resists changing activities when engrossed in own interests
Unusually withdrawn and not active	Preoccupied with own thoughts—daydreamer
Shows extreme behavior (unusually fearful, aggressive, shy or sad)	Deep, intense feelings and reactions

In spite of her perceived social awkwardness, Sara's academic performance was never an issue in kindergarten or any other grade level that followed. Unfortunately, it appears many of our educators are ill-informed and unfamiliar with the wide swath of characteristics that can manifest in a variety of ways and transcend multiple anomalies in student populations. We cannot continue to assume that professional educators are always correct and parents are less equipped to understand their children's learning needs. All children are unique, and each will have his or her own wide range of characteristics! Perhaps Sara's teacher would have been less likely to "categorize" Sara if better understanding of giftedness existed in our schools. Sara had excellent balance riding her horse (at both the walk and jog)! Sara also had no difficulty climbing the Mulberry tree in the front yard or scaling up and over ranch fences and gates! Most parents (their child's advocates) do quite well at diagnosing anomalies they see in their children based on their parental intuition and then seek qualified medical or psychological experts for advice.

Although Sara's classroom experiences were difficult initially, the principal of Sara's elementary school was highly motivated to see each pupil reach his or her highest personal achievements. There was a genuine desire for all students at the school to achieve academic and social success. With the principal's efforts, the staff at Sara's elementary school were soon meeting the individual "advanced-learner" needs that our daughter and several other students required. The school Sara was zoned for and attended was in a blighted area of our rural city. At the time, it had the greatest number of students in our school district who qualified for Title I funds (the disadvantaged and those beneath the poverty line). California had annihilated its budget for education funding, yet Sara's principal continued providing learning opportunities that had been eliminated by budget cuts. It was quite touching to witness the principal greeting the children each morning as they disembarked from school buses. School supplies her pupils needed miraculously appeared. I am certain the "magic, education fairy" was bankrolled by the principal! The leadership of this principal has continued to be a significant influence in forming foundations of lifelong learning in Sara.

By first grade, Sara was given the opportunity to read anything appropriate that she desired. Her teacher encouraged her to read "aloud and proud" to English as a second language (ESL) students who were her classmates. Sara cannot always remember the name of her first-grade teacher, but she does remember being called on to read *Frog and Toad Are Friends* to the first-grade class during an electrical failure (Lobel 1970). Fellow students benefited from hearing English spoken with correct enunciation by someone their own size, and Sara was reading furiously and with sincere enjoyment. She had by this time learned to power herself on the swing set and had readily participated in Junior Olympics (winning the long jump and softball throw). At the same time, Sara had continued to pull significantly ahead of her age/grade peers in academics, and few children played with her at recess or engaged with her at lunchtimes. Her reading, comprehension, vocabulary, and writing abilities prior to kindergarten were reflected in her early primary-grade reports. All areas confirmed Sara's accelerated pace was gaining significant momentum. While shredding old papers in 2013, I had come across Sara's cumulative file. It had been offered to me from her elementary school office when Sara had advanced to middle school. It was lovely to read Sara's sample writings, view her penmanship, and recall her primary learning experiences. While turning pages in the file, I came across her second-grade teacher's assessment of her. "Sara's reading speed was 192 words per minute" and she was "reading at the level of a fifth grader after the ninth month of the school year." This same report to school administration had recommended "Sara should be targeted for Gifted and Talented Education (GATE) acceptance." Sadly, in California, GATE programs do not begin until fourth grade. The instructor had also noted, "I could have moved Sara up to third grade, but I felt it important to see if there were gaps in her learning. There were not." Unbeknownst to us, the early elementary grades had been the beginning of educational frustration that would continue to rise up in Sara. Sara's instructors had all been taught the same teaching methods. For years her educators in our public schools continued to hold fast to their beliefs that "grade skipping" was a bad route to take. The most common reasons I had been presented with were:

1. Grade skipping places younger pupils among older students and exposes them to more mature "inappropriate" behaviors.
2. Grade skipping takes an *A* student (at grade level) and presents much harder challenges, therefore making students work for *C* or *B* marks.

3. It is important to have youngsters maintain "socialization with their age/grade peers."

At that time, I still possessed some trust in some teaching professionals' opinions directing our daughter's education. Our focus had been on Sara receiving a positive educational experience. We believed (once beyond kindergarten) that Sara's elementary school administration and staff were providing that. Sara had continued through the wide alley of normal public education.

Beginning in third grade and through the end of the fifth grade, teachers placed a folder on Sara's classroom desk containing advanced work. Sara was able to access her ability-level challenges as soon as her "seatwork" at grade level had been completed. This allowed her to have at her fingertips information that was intriguing to her. It was a small and inexpensive accommodation that allowed Sara to complete grade-level assignments at her own pace and also to move forward with more difficult challenges at her own ability level. This was an alternative to the widely frowned on "grade skipping" and a working system for Sara during public-school primary grades. Teachers and staff had grown to accommodate her rapid pace, and there was a willingness to work with other accelerated learners in their classrooms as well. Although they had not yet met the minimum fourth-grade requirement, two students (including Sara) had completed all other requirements and had won their school district's reading contest. These students fell between the cracks of policy as "The Battle of the Books" was not designed to include third graders. School staff worked with our county's superintendent of schools office to see that these students were able to participate at the county level in spite of their younger ages and lower grade level. Why would anyone want to thwart the higher reading achievements of capable youngsters? The ability to compete at the county level in a challenge recalling facts in books she had read was wonderful reinforcement for Sara that it was becoming acceptable to learn "outside the box" and beyond age/grade-level standards. For the remainder of her years of primary grade attendance, at her blighted-area public school, Sara continued to develop a foundation of academic confidence and excellence well beyond her age/grade levels.

During her primary years of attendance at Pierce Elementary School, the principal and our daughter had formed their own private lending library. Sara has never forgotten borrowing her principal's book where she first met "Lucy." Lucy was the cause of our first desperate trip to an out-of-town bookstore. Sara absolutely had to own *The Ballad of Lucy Whipple* (in hardcover) for her permanent personal library! (Cushman 1996) Years later, Sara lent Lucy to her older sister, who left the ballad in the rain by accident. This unexpected and devastating loss resulted in a special emergency replacement order of Lucy and a "paperback loans only" rule for the sister! On Sunday, June 1, 2008, Sara placed a book review online at a blog site we had created, www. sarasbookwormreviews.blogspot.com. She hoped her reviews would encourage others to enjoy reading too. All books were rated on a scale of one to five "bookworms" with five being best. A truly excellent book received "five bookworms wearing glasses" (since Sara herself wears glasses). Sara was eight years old when she wrote the following review.

The Ballad of Lucy Whipple

Lucy Whipple, explains how California Morning Whipple (she changes her name to Lucy Whipple) moves with her family from Massachusetts to California. Her brother almost drowns in the river and she is miserable without her father. At first they live in tents but then they build houses of wood. Her brother dies. A fire burns the town and her mother decides to remarry and go to the Sandwich Islands, but Lucy is determined to go back to Massachusetts (until she decides to stay in the town). I liked that she likes books (Like me!). I rate this book 5 bookworms wearing glasses.

Very soon, Sara's reading speed exceeded 238 wpm with 100 percent fluency and accuracy. We sought new avenues to keep pace with an inquisitive and developing mind whose comprehension was phenomenal. Sara's choice of reading material in the upper primary grades had advanced into areas even I had a difficult time embracing. During summer vacation to the beach she had chosen to read, *Kids Are Americans Too* by Bill O'Reilly (O'Reilly 2007). I have never considered the subject of constitutional rights as pleasure reading for any vacation I have ever taken, at any age, let alone as a fourth grader! On Wednesday, August 5, 2009, Sara posted the following review on her blog site. She was nine years old.

Kids Are American's Too

I rated this book '4.5 bookworms' because it is very hard to get into. This book teaches you about your rights - rights that you have as an American citizen. It also teaches you about judges and the Supreme Court. I love the Interlude of Ranting on page nine. I like the quizzes in the book and the Breaking News sections because they were fun. I like that I passed all the quizzes because it means I learned what O'Reilly was trying to teach me. I especially liked the sections called "Ask O'Reilly Special Feature" because they were funny and page 98 tells the reader that we all have to obey the laws and O'Reilly gives us a definition of Anarchy if we don't! I didn't know who Brittney Spears or Angelina Jolie were so I had to ask my mom. There were some words that were new for me. I learned from O'Reilly that my Principal, Mrs. Barnes, can make us wear school uniforms; not wear armor or bring weapons to school; and Principals are the boss because someone has to decide when my rights or your rights are not the best for the whole school! This book was difficult for me in the serious sections. When you are in the core of the apple you can't chew through it very fast. I would recommend this book to Middle School and High School students.

Also at age nine, Sara read a school library book that informed her that Russian students must take a minimum of six years of foreign language beginning in the fifth grade (most study English). Sara wondered why she, now an American fifth-grade student, could not learn Russian in our schools. It seemed to me a foreign language was a reasonable area of study and deserving reasonable access to instruction. Sara's college experience began when her supportive elementary school principal signed off on Sara's first concurrent enrollment form. At the tender age of nine years, our daughter became the youngest pupil ever to enroll at our local California community college. This opportunity for enrichment was not without its preliminary evaluations and its restrictions. I was required to attend an interview with the community college president where the concerns for our child in an adult learning environment were discussed with me (a parent of children in their mid- and late-twenties). The possible detriments of placing Sara in an adult arena were explained. These included what Sara might overhear (adult language and conversations) and oversee (perhaps public displays of affection by same-sex couples). It goes without saying that nine-year-olds are not a common sighting on a college campus full of adults of all ages. Without a doubt, not all very young students are mature enough to handle the adult student-body environment. I'm certain the college administrators were concerned about the potential liability issues. Certainly parents should be wary of placing their children in environments where their safety may be compromised or their childhood innocence sacrificed by exposure to education subjects and materials they are not yet mature enough to process. We should all be discouraging students from copying inappropriate language and MTV dance moves at home and displaying them on grade-school playgrounds and/or in school talent shows. The bumping and grinding dance moves and lyrics spewing sexual innuendo have replaced tetherball courts (now too dangerous to have on primary-school playgrounds). In spite of the reasoning applied by the community college president, I was unable to validate the possible detriments of Sara attending her evening instruction in elementary Russian. On the one hand, college students incur expensive tuition and fees and have paid for costly textbooks to take coursework. They may have strange body piercings, exhibit public displays of same-sex affection, or engage in conversations not appropriate for younger students. On the other hand, Sara had already witnessed her age/grade schoolmates exhibiting disrespect for authority and singing lyrics they had memorized from MTV (inappropriate language uncensored), and many of her age/ grade peers were regularly mimicking popular "bootylicious" dance moves. My husband and I were comfortable with Sara taking a college-level foreign language course that interested her and confident that she would enjoy the learning challenge. My response during my interview was, "It is an elementary Russian language course and not a drawing class with live male nude models. I think she'll be okay."

By the fifth grade, Sara had already recognized that she was different from other children. She noticed that her hobbies and interests were different than those of other children at her school. Having conversations with others her age was stressful for her. She did not know who Hannah Montana was and could not mimic Justin Bieber. School awards programs that recognize students for their achievements had become more difficult for her. Assemblies made her feel unusual, awkward, and weird. Our student felt self-conscious about standing out as the leader in subject achievement. She had learned that standing out for being a "bookworm" or a "super smart" student was *not* an avenue to inclusion on the playground. Being singled out for top honors had become a negative rather than a positive, where the end result was that other children increased their avoidance in playing with her. It was not self-esteem building to be chosen last for team games or to be ignored invitation to participate with classmates at all. Sara had discovered she was never invited to weekend playdates, birthday parties, or sleepovers as her classmates were. Her reaction was to delve into books by using her public-library card more often. She began to develop advanced computer skills using programs at home in her room. She studied plant science independently, viewing seeds, leaves, and fungus under her microscope. Sara had grown quieter, more serious, more studious, and less social in spite of the fact that six and a half hours of every day she was surrounded by age/grade peers. She had attended all the primary grades of public school where the age/grade-level-based education had in fact proved to increase her feelings of being "different," and in her own mind different was a bad thing. In the environment where many education experts believe vital socialization is provided to children and this socialization is necessary both psychologically and emotionally, our child was actually being silently harmed. With exception of the few adults Sara trusted would not consider her "weird," she actively avoided mentioning her attendance in her college night course to others.

Sara's horse had become her best friend. Many mornings before school, I would find her feeding carrots and conversing with the gelding in the yard. One day I asked from the window of my idling truck, "Are you telling him a secret?" and she replied, "Mom! He already knows all my secrets." While this was endearing, it was also very sad. My daughter did not have a single childhood girlfriend to confide in, and the chances of developing a close friendship seemed less likely as time passed. In our ignorance, it had appeared to us that Sara had been happy in her elementary-school environment. In actuality she had not. Her age/grade peers had already withdrawn from her. She frequently sat alone on a swing, reading a book at recess while the other children played together. Sara had not often displayed a confident, extroverted persona with her age group, yet she leaped with vigor into discussions with adults on matters of science and religion. When with her so-called peers, Sara projected an introverted, quiet, and almost nonverbal demeanor, except when asked directly to contribute, assist, or explain a specific subject area. Most days Sara continued to spend her lunchtime in the library, reading silently. It was Sara's most comfortable place and where the school librarian had become one of her fondest few friends. Sara plodded along through the school days and participated in activities but never aligned with the interests of her age/grade peers. Each year the elementary school held a costume parade at Halloween. The children came dressed as ninjas, fairies, Spider-Man, [1] Harry Potter and Hermione Granger, [2] and famous athletes—especially soccer stars! Sara had me assembling white vinyl and foam into her costume—the egg-

---

[1] Spider-Man is a copyright and registered TM of Marvel Comics
[2] Harry Potter and Hermione Granger are registered copyrights and TM of J.K. Rowling, Bloomsbury, Scholastic Press, Warner Bros., and Time Warner

shaped "Extraterrestrial Vegetation Evaluator" (EVE) from the movie Wall-E. [3] Another year, Sara had me purchasing a wig, dyeing, cutting, and styling it. She was determined to dress for the school's Halloween costume parade as an impersonation of her school librarian, Elaine Lopresti. With great surprise and joy, Mrs. Lopresti remarked that she felt honored Sara had impersonated her. This made Sara quite happy too. Her age/grade peers, however, found Sara quite odd to be dressing as their librarian and even more so the year she had dressed as an egg-shaped EVE! The children Sara's age and grade levels often talked in school about birthday parties they had celebrated. There were swimming pool parties, bounce houses, and parties with games, noise makers, and cakes. When asked how she would like to celebrate her birthday during fourth grade, Sara thought about it and said she wanted her classmates to attend an "Earth Day" schoolyard cleanup party and then go for pizza afterward. She had remarked, "Going to my school reminds me of when Daddy and I go to the dump (landfill)." The wind had blown trash along the schoolyard's perimeter fence. There was not a huge acceptance to the invitation to come clean up garbage for her birthday! The following year Sara held her tenth birthday party in the middle of the children's section of the local bookstore. The children played a game that matched book characters to book titles. The cake design was an open book, and rather than sending her guests home with bags of treats, each received a bookstore gift certificate. The same three schoolmates had attended each birthday

---

[3] Wall-E is a registered copyright and TM of Pixar Studios, and Disney

event (each with younger siblings who came along). Sara has had no interest in further birthday celebrations. She was by her very nature set apart from the average or "normal" age/grade peer who had idolized an athlete, warlock, or popular superhero, and her birthdays did not involve streamers and balloons, boisterous youngsters, or loud activities. We had come to accept that Sara was nothing like our other children. It had become increasingly obvious she was also not like *any* children, especially those who were her age/grade peers. Years later, Sara explained that she had always felt she was unlike other children.

It should cause the heart of any mother to ache when made aware of the degree their youngster had felt "bullied" by their own age/grade peers. I was horrified to hear Sara explain years later, "It wasn't physical like pushing—it was alienation." At the time, I had noticed that Sara migrated to specific adults at her elementary school and excitedly looked forward to conversations with those adults each school day. What I did not understand *then* was our very young child had already begun meeting her own need for intellectual stimulation and socialization. The conversations Sara had been having with her principal and librarian, rather than the children her age and grade level with whom she had little in common, were a way of meeting her own advanced needs requirements. It was disturbing to *now* learn our daughter had felt condemned to endure so many days and years of alienation from other youngsters and just how long Sara had thought herself a "freak of nature."

THREE

The Beauty of Creation

Parent's concerned about their own children's education performances had regularly asked me, "What did you do to make Sara so smart?" My answer was, "Nothing." We didn't make Sara smart. She was born the way she is—just like all our other children were born the way they are too. We have not been remiss in parenting when our children enacted their God-given free will to go against our advice. As well, we are not interested in claiming credit when our children have used their free will to pursue their God-given purposes, have developed their own God-given abilities, or have achieved goals by their own efforts. Nothing we did *made* Sara smart. We didn't give her any special smoothies, vitamins, or diet restrictions. We didn't keep her isolated from germs or avoid recommended vaccinations. We didn't run an air-purification system in her room, pump in extra oxygen, or feed her wheat germ, kale, and lemon grass. Sara had her share of refined sugars and gluten, and sometimes I forgot to buy the dairy products from cows *not* treated with hormones. Sometimes Sara slept with horse-event germs (when exhaustion took precedence over bathing), and she has always been the most healthy of all our children.

What we *did* do was to give a curious mind the means to contemplate and reason answers to questions she had. We happened to be raising a child who loved to learn—about everything! Naturally, we wanted to promote this enjoyable passion our daughter had. There were ways that we provided inexpensive and readily available activities at home to keep Sara's enthusiasm fed. However, if we had provided nothing at all, Sara's intellectual abilities would still be what they are (though likely less developed while waiting on growth opportunities). We wanted Sara to have various avenues to engage in learning, to develop knowledge unobstructed, and to have opportunities to choose study subjects that interested her and therefore were a pleasure for her to learn about.

Fiction and nonfiction reading provide benefits to comprehension in different ways. At younger ages, every book interested Sara. Once I had discovered that nonfiction books could provide comprehension growth related to dates, names, timelines, and historical events while also providing interesting reading material that Sara would find pleasurable and engaging, I suggested Sara read biographies of women in science, space exploration, military service, education, music, and the arts. I paid more attention to how many fiction books Sara had read versus nonfiction books. I would suggest true-life stories that might (or perhaps not) be of interest to her. Sara has a public-library card and a book bag designated solely for the county library, and they have been well used over the years. I don't believe it is enough to *promote* reading. I think all parents (of gifted children or not) should engage their children in conversation about the details of what they have read. I believe having a conversation with children, face to face, about their reading materials encourages true contemplation about written materials they have read. Conversations give children valuable time to practice their communication skills while conveying what they comprehended from their books. Most important, it shows that parents value their children enough to sit down without their cell phones and have a discussion with the human beings their children are! It is astounding to me just how many parents are "too busy" to talk with their child at length.

What we also did was to enable Sara's enjoyment in areas of learning that were her interest already. If she read a book about a painter, we got out the watercolors, and she painted. I know I enjoyed our "Artist for a Day" trips to the base of Mt. Whitney, California, where we painted pictures of the trees in hues of blue greens, and the Lone Pine Creek as it trickled by, almost unnoticed. If math homework problems involved money, we dumped out the piggy bank and went shopping to see how close to zero we could get without hitting a minus number. Sometimes the piggy bank purchased a single scoop of ice cream, and sometimes it was a chocolate sundae! Learning can be fun, and valuable learning opportunities do not solely take place in the classroom of a professional educator. Valuable lessons do not require a lot of cash. Time to interact with Sara was what she required from me. Books (fiction or nonfiction) came to life, exposing meaning and purpose to the subject through experience. Even if the experiences were snippets of time and our conversations brief, the gaining of new knowledge had utmost importance in Sara's world!

Sara has been given time and space to process the information she has garnered. She has not changed from that small kindergartner who knew her personal-space boundaries and still prefers her quiet time alone. While alone, she has contemplated, absorbed, and mulled over subject materials. Then, when she has sufficiently processed, she has shared her opinions with us. It has been interesting to hear why Sara has found some information horrible, hysterical, historical, a must read, or a keep-forever volume. Equally entertaining have been her explanations on why a book was tossed in the donation box and she never, ever, wanted to read it *ever* again! In order for Sara to better process what she had learned and clearly convey information to others, she and I (with help from Lance Sanchez) had earlier created her online blog for book reviews. This was an avenue to improve Sara's writing abilities, bring out of her memory her favorite details of the books she had read, practice keyboarding, and receive comments from her blog followers (though few people actually participated as followers). At her young age, the process was initially fun. She eventually outgrew the activity but not before her exposure to computer use and development of keyboarding skills (that assisted her later on with being prepared for concurrent enrollment in college courses).

Long before we suspected Sara was on a supersonic track of educational development, the very first thing my husband and I did for her was to kill our TV! It's true; we have not had television programming fed in to our home since the year 2000—that means no MTV. Sara has had no video-gaming system—ever! I regret I did not do this when my older children were still young. I was younger then too and not as wise to the influence and detriment of children being "plugged in" to constant entertainment by media. I apologize to all our elder children for this (although I'm sure they are grateful for my oversight with their Atari[4] and Nintendo[5] games). Sara also had no Bratz Dolls[6] and no toy electronic animals to feed when their keychain alarms went off. We did not purchase our daughter an Emoto-Tronic Furby[7] (although 27 million of the popular Hasbro Furby toys had sold in a single twelve-month period). Sara was not absorbed by pop or rap music on an MP3 player or an iPod[8] that she did not own. She also had no need for a cell phone (with or without texting). Sara's early childhood was viewed as odd by today's standards—not unlike the way our modern American society views the Amish of Lancaster, Pennsylvania, who continue living in the "old" ways. Instead of watching television sitcoms Sara spent her valuable free time reading the next in a favorite series of books, riding her horse or bicycle, absorbing sunshine and pruning trees with her father in his hobby orchard, or running electric trains in a maze under her bed and out of her bedroom door. She also had ample time to design and build her own roller coasters and to build various items using skill saws, jig saws, and other power tools in her father's garage. When it came to Earth science, Sara has had a microscope with interesting slides as well as

---

[4] Atari logo, games and systems are a TM and copyright of Atari Inc., and/or Infogrames

[5] Nintendo logo, games and gaming systems are a TM and copyright of Nintendo and Nintendo of America

[6] Bratz Dolls are a TM and copyright of MGA Entertainment, Inc.

[7] All Furby logos, characters, and models are a TM and copyright owned by Hasbro and/or Tiger Electronics

[8] iPod is a registered TM of Apple Computers, Inc.

blank slides to collect her own earth-science samples. She has (with her dad's supervision) collected various disgusting live things in glass jars (scorpions, black widows, and sun spiders) for observation. Sara has spent many hours in self-directed learning adventures.

Heaven forbid I forget to mention the annual return of Sara's wild gopher snake that at times appears in the garage or in a flower pot on the garden patio. This year it reappeared slithering up a tree outside Sara's bedroom window to dine on recently hatched baby birds (in the wooden birdhouse Sara had made years prior). I'm not sure how Sara and her father know it is the same gopher snake, but perhaps they have put a name bracelet on it. Sara has named her reappearing reptile Phillip, but I cannot bring myself to exclaim, "Sara! Look! Phillip has reappeared!" I annually insist she and her father get it away from *my* house! Phillip should not be confused with local treacherous snakes—the Mojave red racer, Mojave green, and Western diamondback rattlesnake—that are seldom seen on our property. I assure myself the absence of the venomous varieties is due to our free-range chickens. The poultry birds have not been ranging free for several years (since the coyotes discovered where to get "run-through" chicken dinner). It gives me false comfort, believing the venomous snakes are unaware the chickens are now caged birds. Obviously, this assumes snakes possess a "higher-level reasoning," which is not my point. I don't truly think vector or vermin intelligence quotients are in the "gifted ranges." I am actually citing my own attempt to rationalize why I don't need to worry about going outside my own door. Smart snakes would remain slithering outside the boundary line of our property (and never migrate inside the wire fencing) to avoid being eaten by our poultry birds. Snake self-preservation is no doubt a poor line of logic on my part, an obvious overreach in presuming venomous-reptile reasoning abilities. In any case, the time Sara has spent in self-directed study of nature and observing desert wildlife has been valuable. It has included learning about the endangered desert tortoise that migrated through her grandfather's property line, the quail and roadrunners that quickly snatched the grain and hay leaf dropped by our horses, doves nesting on the ground, coyotes stealthily preying, jackrabbits, cottontails, and as much as I had been repulsed by them, the creepy insects in glass containers housed in Dad's garage! Again, education does not solely take place in classroom settings. It is not always directed by credentialed teachers. Sara has learned many valuable things on her own and in the absence of age/grade-peer socialization.

Sara has also had access to some remarkable adults who have mentored her. Years ago my husband introduced Sara to a coworker from the Southwest. Adults might describe Lance Sanchez as a "guru of technology" or perhaps a "binary man in tune with his code." I'm not really certain what powers Lance's stimulated mind, but to our daughter he has been like Maria's fantastic godfather, Drosselmeyer (a clockmaker and inventor) from *The Nutcracker and the Mouse King* (Hoffmann 1816). Only, at Christmases in our house, Lance brought our daughter a build-your-own-robotics robot kit (increasing her discovery of mechanical and electrical engineering, and computer science). Lance also brought our child things that flew through my house, exposing Sara to the fabulous adventures in dining room aerodynamics, and other advanced technological toys for fast-absorbing minds. I occasionally still find little plastic rabbits in our home that were made by Lance's computer-generated, tabletop electronic machinery that intrigued Sara. Actually, I think my dentist used the same machine recently to create a crown on demand for my cracked molar. All these "Lance things" were *magical* and so much better than any wooden nutcracker prince. Still, none of these Godfather Drosselmeyer influences made our daughter smart. What they did was to provide her curious mind with opportunities for exploration. They also eliminated distractions (sedentary entertainment) that had no tangible or useful benefits to someone very young and easily influenced. Why would a child want to watch aerodynamic cartoons on television when they could be thrilled flying a new gift from Lance into Mom's chandelier? Sara's room, like other children's, is full of treasures. Many are self-propelled, remote controlled, battery, or electric powered. Some have glass parts, metal parts, or time consuming "assembly required." None is a doll of any kind. Sara's interest in dolls was brief—about two weeks in her life. All the dolls in the house are mine. "How-to" science-experiment books and engineering manuals—those are hers!

I have always wanted all our children to become well-rounded, knowledgeable, educated, happy adults who would be successful in ascertaining God's purpose for their own lives—and go accomplish that purpose. What we did for all our children, including Sara, was to engage their curiosity as they grew and developed. What has been different in raising Sara has been her intuitive understanding, her *own* desire for advanced knowledge at faster rates of speed and the obstructions to her access of those higher-level educational opportunities. Her inquisitive questions have often required me to delay an answer while I researched the topic.

It was impossible to avoid noticing that Sara's childhood was passing by with increasing speed. Her childhood was certainly traveling past us at greater speed than our other children's had. Continuing to pass by Sara were invitations to birthday parties, slumber parties, and swimming pool parties. Sara had by this time created an emotional wall. She no longer felt disappointed at the invitations she never received. She did not expect to receive any invites from the friends she did not have. It was not easy to continuously affirm to Sara that she had been "truly blessed" or explain to her that having received beautiful God-given abilities, it was the responsible thing for her to develop them. As she grew older she began to view herself as "freakish," obviously so *strange* that no other children wanted to engage with her. Children who did engage with Sara usually were instructed to do so for classroom participation and not a desire to establish true friendship with someone whose personal interests had expanded beyond their own understanding and whose academic knowledge had soared as many as six grades beyond their own. Feeling ostracized by her age/grade peers was not helping to convince Sara that God had a purpose for "blessing" her. I believe most parents want their children to have friends. In our culture, playmates are important in childhood. Perhaps in third-world countries, this is a luxury many children go without while they worry if they will be sheltered from weather, have enough clean water, or even live to see tomorrow. Our daughter has not lived in a third-world country. Sara has been spared the concerns facing millions of children in impoverished and war-torn lands. There are many things children face even in America that Sara has been spared. Comparisons to things worse, however, did not change Sara's own situation or improve her self-esteem. Sara's lack of companionship with human friends was having a silent effect on her. Her self-directed and self-paced absorption of knowledge was giving her true pleasure. Simultaneously, it was creating true barriers to human interaction. Her growing solitude often left me worried and deeply concerned about her apparent lonely existence. Girl Scouts, swimming lessons, and dance classes had all grouped children together by age and/or grade level. Other than the scheduled meeting times, lessons, or events as a group, Sara had not been included in those children's parties, movie dates, or sleepovers either. Finding social situations where Sara could feel "alike" and not "different" was proving more and more difficult a challenge. Some people had commented to us about Sara's lack of access to cable television, cellular telephones, and so on. Some even voiced their opinions that we needed to advance into the twenty-first century (including our elder children). My husband earns a comfortable living in (of all things) the field of information technology. I have never felt (as some expressed) that we "deprived" Sara by living without cable television or Wii[9] or in a home without a paved street access, curbs, or gutters. I rather think it has been a better choice to raise our family under the light of the stars

---

[9] Wii is a registered TM held by Nintendo

and away from the bright lights of the city. It has been nice to be away from the noise of the neighbors' arguments and instead to be within earshot of the coyote's howling. No doubt it has also been less expensive—Sara did not see all the commercial advertisements on television and think she would die if we didn't buy whatever the advertisement was selling. I do feel Sara was deprived of some things. Specifically, she should have had more enjoyable learning hours in the classrooms instead of struggling against ridged education policies that restrict students based on age and grade level. Sara was deprived of what could have been a more pleasant and enriched formal education experience. Eventually, Sara's father (on his own terms) had supplied her with all the modern information-technology gadgets: the inevitable MP4 player and the personal computer (with parental controls) on which she reads book reviews, plays games, creates art and computerized animation, and performs college-level course work. Her gadgets have recently been upgraded to systems far beyond my own technology levels. Sara also has a Kindle[10] that is dusty and seldom moves from the shelf where it lives. Lucy's hard cover, however, is still well loved! I've often asked Sara if she would like to put more books on her e-reader, but she consistently replies, "Real books are real. They aren't a bunch of black things on a screen. You don't have to wait for the page to load, and you don't need to create a bookmark for every page you like—you just go there." I think that means, "No thanks, Mom," and also explains why a fifth bookcase is now required in the girl's "cave."

---

[10] Kindle is a registered TM of Amazon.com

The growing intellectual needs required by Sara remained strange territory for my husband and me. At ten years old, our youngster had pulled down a passing grade in a college-level Elementary Russian class. How does one raise such a child? Scarier still, as fifth grade neared an end, the advancement to middle school was inevitable. We knew the provisions for higher academic challenges that had been made for our child would change. In the stable environment of her elementary school, Sara had felt supported by teachers and staff. She may not have made lasting friendships with other children, but she had felt secure. As parents, determining the best education decisions to make for Sara in the near future was very disconcerting. How did we know if we were meeting her needs appropriately? When was too much too soon? What was too little or too late? Advocating for Sara at this time was much more difficult than ever. Promoting a loyal relationship with her friend "Lucy" and supporting the emotional bonding Sara had with her horse in the yard was easy. But conveying to Sara that other "real" children, their parents, middle-school teachers, and others within our community were also kind and accepting, Sara was not buying that! She had retreated into believing there were no others *like her* or even others who would be accepting of her. Sara's maturity level (at that time) convinced her that she knew why other children did not want to play with her and had excluded her in their activities. She had a heart and mind that viewed herself as *"just too different"* to be accepted, and therefore her abilities were a curse rather than a blessing. I too felt there were few human cheerleaders within my own peer group, supporting *me* from the sidelines as I tried to discover what was best for Sara and as we attempted to navigate this very different child raising experience.

Sometimes, to be effective as a child advocate, you may eventually conclude, "When in need, create!" I was soon the founding community leader of the Ridgerunners 4-H Club. There were certain requirements in setting up a 4-H club and one caused me to draft Sara's high school–age sister, Emma, to serve as the founding club president. As a parent, it was validating to see how willing our older daughter was to meet a need that might result in her sister developing friendships. Emma maintained her own commitments to coursework, marching band, madrigals choir, and yearbook photographer for her high school. She also showed up regularly and conducted the monthly Ridgerunners 4-H Club general meetings (wearing what most high school students think is "that goofy 4-H hat"). 4-H involvement did in fact prove to be a good social environment for Sara. The 4-H Youth Development Program is structured in a way that allowed Sara to be accepted by her age peers. Grade levels and academic achievements mean little to youth in 4-H. Youth learn many nongraded life skills. Some learn leadership. All participate in community service projects. Others learn to ride a horse, to show a dog, to raise a market lamb, or to become better public speakers. All learn the importance of developing healthy lifestyle choices. All 4-H members learn to work as a team, as a club, in unison for the greater good in planning their club's participation in local activities. Sara enjoyed being in parades and attending club parties, and she was comfortable pursuing activities with children sharing related interests. Grade level and grade-point averages were irrelevant. This had proven to be a good choice of social interaction with other youth. It was also an area for challenging, new learning activities. Most importantly, it was an environment where academic performance was not normally the conversation topic! The 4-H Cooperative Youth Development Program has been a wonderful opportunity for Sara to have experienced acceptance by other youth. Children were engaging with her for who she was; her "different" personality did not often dissuade interactions. Hobbies and learning interests were an excellent common ground. Youth were far more interested in Sara's horsemanship skills and her faithful, trusted mount, "Catch," than they were with her reading level! Few mentions were made about standardized test scores or performances on exams. Sara, now a cautiously guarded ten-year-old, was slowly warming to this *new* experience of having friends!

We have known some very competitive families where children are channeled and encouraged toward competitive academic contests and competitive sports. Sara's character, whether instinctive or learned, avoided areas where she was singled out. We saw this in extracurricular activities such as her equestrian events and 4-H club involvement. Sara was not motivated by garnering the blue, first-place ribbon against an equestrian competitor, but in the pleasure of riding her own horse with improved skill. She was not vying for the top award as a Ridgerunners 4-H Club public speaker or as a club officer, but she was enjoying her participation in agricultural projects where the goal was do her personal best. Sara preferred participation in community service projects to competitions pitting her against others. In every aspect of her chosen extracurricular activities, Sara had pursued self-improvement and not the limelight of being recognized "best," which would single her out from the majority. At school, however, Sara continued dealing with being a social outcast, and academic boredom was increasing. With middle school inevitable, we were hopeful Sara would have accepting friends from 4-H to associate with, as sixth grade quickly approached. I attempted to memorize, "Do not fear, for I am with you; Do not anxiously look about you, for I am your God. I will strengthen you, surely I will help you, Surely I will uphold you with My righteous right hand" (Isaiah 41:10 NASB).

FOUR

The Eye of the Storm

Most parents rejoice when their child advances out of elementary school. We met the change with trepidation. Shortly after being advanced from her supportive environment into the larger pupil-attendance numbers of the middle school grades, our reality hit home. Middle-school accommodations for accelerated learners was limited to a few subject opportunities in a student's current grade. In sixth grade, English honors was available. The following year, seventh grade English honors and math honors would be permitted. Sara could take a geometry course in the eighth grade. The explanation or reasoning for our school district's limited advanced programming was, "Ninth-grade geometry builds upon eighth-grade introductory algebra, which builds upon seventh grade math." After repeated conversations with the education staff, we understood the school district's philosophy.

- Educators do not want pupils to have "gaps" in learning from grade skipping or from subject acceleration.
- Teachers are already struggling with great learning diversities in their classrooms.
- Education administrators do not want to impact overburdened teachers with further disparity by

having them prepare individual lesson plans for advanced learners.

- When a child enters a classroom too highly advanced, it impacts a teacher's planned curriculum, which they do not have time to change.
- Experienced educators believe it is best to teach grade-level concepts at age/grade appropriate periods of time.

My husband and I and our daughter clung to our optimistic attitudes that sixth grade would be a positive experience! Sadly, it was not.

Sara experienced a rapid decline in motivation to attend school. She deliberately "dumbed down" to a poorer achievement than her proven abilities. We watched Sara as she became increasingly sullen and withdrawn. When addressing these changes with her principal, I was told, "She's probably one of those students who is just having a difficult time making the adjustment to middle school." The principal had no interest in taking our concerns seriously. Rather, she had quickly disregarded our child's specific needs and issues, choosing instead to group our child into a common response given parents: "Your child is maturity deficient." At home the detrimental effects the sixth-grade experience was having on our daughter were more visible each week. I persisted in my concern for adequate challenges for our student and was told, "She must not be *that* gifted since she's not making As." Clearly we, her advocates, had reached impasse with the administrator of the middle school for which Sara was zoned. The state of California had given our local school district (and every school district in the state) the right to self-govern. In turn, our school district had passed to each school's administrator the authority to determine the breadth and scope of any Gifted and Talented Education (GATE) program at the school over which an administrator was in charge. Few options for combating this solid educational brick wall existed. The public middle school administrator had determined GATE opportunities were both "enrichment" and "parents' responsibility." To make matters further compounded, our local community college had also undergone "priority-enrollment" changes. There was now a series of registration delays before Sara could enroll in any evening "enrichment" through community college courses. Sara would have to wait for the priority students (veterans, children of veterans, foster care students); regular adult-enrollment students, high school seniors, and finally high school juniors before she could attempt to register for a course—which was not wait-listed. Sara was not permitted to wait-list any classes. The middle school had staunchly refused to allow Sara into more difficult courses and had taken the stance that we as parents should provide the appropriate level of educational "enrichment" for Sara, but simultaneously, the college had produced an effective barrier to Sara's enrollment in those enrichment opportunities. It appeared we could do little to promote a better public-school learning situation— one in which our daughter could again thrive.

After hearing many conflicting opinions from our local educators regarding Sara's abilities—or lack of abilities— we no longer trusted our local school district educators or officials. These same professionals were stuck on their belief in the importance of Sara to socialize with her "age/grade peers." They viewed this socialization as a huge impact on her life, both then and in the future. A serious problem was the inability of these school officials to witness what was really going on—also known as "they couldn't see the forest for the trees." The pain Sara was experiencing was as clear to us as her school's blindness to it. Among other things, her peers had called her a "brainiac, bookworm, nerd, geek, and dork." A host of mean and inappropriate barbs were regularly hurled at her by the very peers school officials thought so important to her well-being. Officials would not have tolerated racial epithets, disparaging gender comments, or the bullying of disabled students, but they ignored what they considered "normal" language Sara's peers spoke to her on the quad during the pass times to the next class. It was worrisome to see educators turn a deaf ear and a blind eye to their own "zero tolerance policy" when it came to the studious and eager learner who was far advanced for her age. Sara's middle school peers were interested in discussing the latest television sitcoms and viewing contemporary music videos. Sara continued to spend the majority of her time pursuing her individual interests (usually in the serenity of a library). She continued exploring academics far above her grade level. Teachers themselves inadvertently added to Sara's feeling that she *"didn't belong."* In one class, our daughter assisted a failing student because she had already mastered the course work and beyond. This freed the teacher to assist others and meet the mandate of pupils achieving grade-level standards, and it was a wonderful opportunity for the failing student to receive dedicated assistance. While this gave Sara something to do with her class-time boredom, it did nothing to advance or challenge the ability levels of Sara. Assisting her failing classmate was kind and helpful, but it did not provide Sara with an intriguing, interesting, or challenging new learning opportunity. Here again was an example portraying Sara as that *"super smart"* student while also increasing the divide between her and her age/grade peers. Numerous meetings with school officials could not change the status quo. Teachers were not prepared to offer accelerated curriculum that deviated from their prepared lesson plans. Sara's difficulty socializing with age/grade peers grew. Restricted access to higher-level opportunities and educational advancement combined with a lack of school friends contributed to the onset of depression. Sara's academic performance fell, and her motivation to attend school died while enduring hours of monotonous compulsory boredom.

Establishing social connections with age/grade-level peers was a goal of the past. It was now ridiculous to promote such an ideal. In that large, "normal" environment, Sara was *different*, and to public middle school students, different *is* "weird!" Sara's age/grade compulsory education was no longer a good match for her academic requirements or for any social interaction. For two semesters, she was prevented from attending college courses in the evenings. Sara did not always know how to react to her differences, but she was expressing more frustration at being forced to attend school at all. As the year progressed, so did the frequency of her statement, "I don't want to go to school. I'm tired of being a freak!" As a mother this was a heartbreaking statement to hear. No parent wants to hear agony in their young child's voice. As a parent I did not understand the full breadth and scope of giftedness, but any reasonably attentive parent would have been able to identify his or her child drifting into dangerous and angry territory. Parents are not always able to assess the educational special needs specific to their children or find the alternative accommodations their children might need. In Sara's case, we continually sought educational doors of opportunity so our child could thrive in subjects at her ability levels, but our success had been made harder to achieve. There were four good things to come out of our daughter's sixth grade school year.

1. Sara had been invited by a girlfriend from 4-H to her very first sleepover.
2. After waiting for priority and regular-enrollment student registration, few had chosen to enroll in the college Elementary Russian II course, so there was an available seat for Sara.
3. Sara's oral presentation to her 4-H Club members on the Cyrillic alphabet and basic greetings in Russian helped earn her the 4-H bronze-star rank.
4. I was more determined than ever to discover the needs our child had so we could meet them.

I had reached the point where I distrusted nearly every local educator's "esteemed" opinion on the direction he or she thought we should take with Sara. Family and friend's opinions too were often ill informed. Initially, I felt insulted by comments made by those who believed they had a valid and factual basis. As our journey had progressed, I continually felt like the lone soldier on the battlefield for gifted education.

What was the true meaning of "gifted?" Why was it bandied about erroneously? What path should we take with our child from this point forward? I wanted what Sara did—her opportunity to develop her academic strengths. She did not need to be held captive under the law in an environment that stifled her. What she needed was to receive her own legally guaranteed "appropriate education." We simply had no idea what was "appropriate." Just how intellectually intuitive was our youngster? Was she gifted but not *that* gifted, as some educators had declared? Did she really require a substantially different education than our other four children had received in the same public school system? Was Sara both bright and having an "adjustment problem" to middle school? Some had even suggested my husband and I invoke stronger discipline, citing that our daughter was clearly capable of making better grades and was choosing to be a slacker. Disciplining a withdrawn and unhappy child would hardly have been the correct tack to take.

Having lost confidence in local school officials, I sought to have an unbiased psychologist give an IQ test to our daughter. In my ignorance, I thought obtaining proof of a high IQ score was all we needed to get an Individual Education Plan (IEP) in place for Sara within our school district. I telephoned psychologists in our area (there were three), but each had the same answer—"I don't see healthy children. My practice deals with children who are having serious problems." I telephoned our medical insurance for a referral only to discover we didn't have coverage for education evaluations and testing. Our insurance covered only "mental health problems." In my opinion, our daughter's mental health was being negatively affected by peer alienation, self-isolation, and academic boredom. This was a problem! In previous years, I had been comfortable bouncing thoughts and ideas off the elementary school principal, whom I trusted. It was time to take a much stronger approach to meet Sara's current and future educational needs. We required a specialist in the field of giftedness. Where were we going to find an unbiased, knowledgeable and reputable professional to guide us on this increasingly challenging journey? Our rural location is a good environment to raise a family—clean air, untainted water, low crime rate, and a tight-knit community. Overall, there is a wholesomeness that larger urban salaries and convenient access to retail stores just can't buy. Alternatively, our rural location, by its geography, makes education choices severely limited. Opportunities for Sara to interact with others like herself, to participate in activities offered within gifted organizations, or to access experts in giftedness are hundreds of miles away. I needed someone to evaluate, explain, and advise us on an education path that was best for Sara. The daily view of Sara in emotional distress and my own thoughts of her future (perhaps eleven years old on antidepressant medication) were not working for any of us. Six more years of the existing public school education situation was not an option. The mileage required in getting to an expert advisor was not an issue at that point either. I did what any good mother in modern times would do. I turned to *Google!*

While in the Google trenches and seeking to understand our child's educational needs, I read about traits many profoundly gifted individuals share. Initially, I was delighted to read just how "normal" our daughter's quirky mannerisms and habits were when compared to other profoundly or exceptionally gifted youth. I briefly considered sending a complimentary list to several former teachers and education professionals. Those who had disregarded Sara's need for higher challenges and those who had reacted in disbelief that she had actually done her own work at much higher levels than her age/grade peers would certainly have benefited from the research I had done. I was reminded how that "root of bitterness" kept wanting to send out fresh sprigs! The search engine on my laptop became a close friend and research on giftedness a passion. I was in awe of the amount of information I discovered online—for free! Why did school teachers, administrators, and staff not know the proven research I was discovering? Perhaps they did know—and they like it when parents go along blindly and ignorantly! Through the Internet, I finally began to understand my child's frustration and pain because I began to educate myself and to fully understand Sara's personality. Most of my research was jumping from websites where information was repeated in the same proven areas about gifted children. Eventually, I hit upon the website for the Palmer Learning Center that soothed my weary soul! Sara was definitely not a *"freak,"* as she had convinced herself she was. Sara was actually among a small fraction of our population. True gems, they are treasures so rare they are often unseen. These are amazingly unique children, and they do require individualized strategies to meet their special needs. Thanks to the Internet search engine, Google, I found an expert who was qualified to answer our questions and enlighten me about this very different and youngest child of ours. A licensed educational psychologist, Dr. Palmer's specialty includes youngsters just like Sara. Within hours I had received a response to my e-mail inquiry. This is likely the most important e-mail I have ever sent. My husband and I received a packet of information to complete separately, prior to Sara's assessment. As I read the material and looked over the questionnaire, I realized all the small things Sara had done that our four other children had not. Why had I overlooked these things? I had never considered all the small unusual things she had done in the past, or continued to do in the present, were collectively important. I had no idea that many gifted individuals share so many common characteristics. Whichever hand the book is in Sara will always eat dinner with the other. I never gave much thought to Sara's being ambidextrous. Why would I? She had been that way from infancy. Like most parents, we had become accustomed to our child's character traits and in the course of daily life accepted Sara's inherent individuality. There had been so much chaos going on in our blended family of older children we had simply accepted Sara's attributes and run on. I ran to ballet recitals, band concerts, driving tests, graduations, and college visits. I had worried over four children during that endless nightmare experienced by all parents "dating." At times, it had been a relief to have one child who preferred to delve into a good book, content to just be at home, while I was a human GPS-locator tracking teenagers! I had accepted the *quirky* things Sara had done as simply being Sara. I never considered that collectively her traits were clues to an uncommon occurrence that would require us to meet very special needs. What Sara had always displayed were actually common characteristics of profoundly gifted individuals.

As our appointment date with Dr. Palmer approached, so did our anxiety. My husband and I were cranky with each other while driving four hours in freeway traffic only to arrive at what turned into a bad night in a noisy motel. The next morning, my husband ran a credit card through the parking meter across the street from Dr. Palmer's office. We glanced at Sara and knew this was our last chance to back out and run. We were about to send our little girl into the office of a man I had located online—a "headshrinker," no less! Dr. Palmer's reputation and credentials are well documented, but as parents, we were very nervous. We proceeded into his office and were met with a quick greeting, a handshake, and several suggestions of local places to see while we left Sara for a couple of hours. What! We were leaving our young daughter there alone for testing that would take hours to complete—and we weren't even going to be within earshot! Leaving Sara alone behind closed doors with a stranger I located online goes against the grain of parental advice from every source, both oral and written. In all honesty, we were invited to remain in the comfortable lobby if we had wanted to. We are not normally "helicopter parents," prone to hovering. This was an unusual thing we were doing. By far the most compelling reason to go see the local sites was that our daughter wanted us to go away while she was being "assessed." Sara was ready to take any test, fulfill any requirement, or testify before anyone if it meant changing her existing, miserable school experience. She had a bounce in her step as she went toward the testing area around the corner from the lobby while my husband and I sluggishly slid out as far as the parking lot. We sat on the tailgate of our truck and watched the parking meter tick down! No amount of gelato at the beach on a sunny day can make time go by faster in situations like that. It had occurred to us that we might receive information even we were not ready to absorb. It will probably be the only time in our lives we looked forward to a parking meter running out! We jaunted inside to collect our daughter who exited with a smile, stating, "That was fun!" Dr. Palmer smiled and said, "Feed her lunch and bring her back at two o'clock. We have some more to do." I'm sure we looked like we needed to read *How to Relax for Dummies* as we affirmed we had heard and understood. Off we went in search of pizza, returning Sara with blood-sugar and protein levels up, bounding back into Dr. Palmer's office without any anxiety at all. We sheepishly slid the credit card to feed the parking meter again and walked to the nearby beach where we sat and watched the tourists. We were glad Sara was having a good testing experience while we were each processing the what-ifs. What if she's having a barrel of fun because she's really bombing this evaluation and going to be miserable for six more years of school? What if she's not truly high IQ? Do we have an alternative education plan for her? The two hours turned into two and a half and then three. Other parents with their young clients were patiently waiting as their scheduled appointment times passed, yet all were very courteous, and none seemed to mind the wait. As I observed the families, it occurred to me that perhaps they too were tormented parental souls seeking guidance and direction for the children God had also blessed them with.

One youngster was busily entertaining himself in an alcove designed for the young and curious when we were called to join our daughter in the room where she had spent her day. Sara continued to be mesmerized with solving a challenge given to her by Dr. Palmer as he went over his assessments and his preliminary results with us. We finally had confirmation from an unbiased expert. Sara "had not and would not level out." I felt relieved hearing the explanation that Sara "has not learned everything there is to know. Rather she has all the brain power she needs to learn anything she desires to." I was encouraged and grateful for Dr. Palmer's reassuring remarks that my own intuition had been correct. For the first time I felt both confident and validated that my own educational observations and decisions had been well founded. Dr. Palmer's written results would allow us to push forward in meeting the special needs of this child that God had placed in our care. I felt secure and armed, knowing there was now convincing and irrefutable evidence for meeting Sara's "special needs for higher level challenges and advanced learning opportunities." Dr. Palmer's assessments would be evidence that our local school district could not easily shrug off as our being overzealous parents with harmful educational ideas.

I have often referred to my complimentary copy of Dr. Palmer's book, *Parent's Guide to IQ Testing and Gifted Education,* that has helped me to understand the fantastic way Sara's mind works. On the long drive home, I opened the cover to a world full of wonderful explanations about why Sara behaved the way she did, felt the way she did, and responded to situations the way she did. I read the section

"The Flipside to Having a High IQ." I knew we had made the correct decision. I better understood Sara and why she didn't seem interested in things her "normal" age peers were. To her, attaining knowledge was paramount! In her very young mind, it would be a waste of time to brush her hair or be concerned with chocolate ice cream on her chin. Those menial tasks take vital minutes away from what is on the next page of the book she is reading! The hands-on exploration of how she could customize, build, and redesign components in her robotics kit was a much better use of her time than having clean laundry! I had struggled with this fifth child of ours, thinking she exhibited new meaning to the terms "laziness" and "inattention" to simple, ordinary, and daily tasks. Her lack of concern for completing basic tasks had been complete torture for me! In actuality, mundane tasks and chores *are* still necessary, but in Sara's young mind, they were also trivial, and her time was much better spent gleaning new information! To Sara, intriguing subjects, solving problems, or building a better anything was a much better use of her time. I recalled when her father had taken her to task on things beyond my technology levels (which are surprisingly low). It was not enough to know how many songs could be compressed on an MP4 player without becoming distorted; Sara spent time discovering at what compression rates different genres of music became distorted. Reading Dr. Palmer's book, my "aha light" had finally come on. Sara was not stubborn; she was searching. She was not difficult; she was discovering. She was not in her room "socially isolated"; she was actually "introspective" (Palmer, 117).

Sara's domain is a true reflection of her priorities. The bed is tolerated. She could do without having a chest of drawers since she views clothes as required to protect herself from the elements and nothing more. Therefore, few clothing options are required. "Jeans and a T-shirt Mom. Mom! I'm good with jeans and T-shirt." Fashion is not only absent from her radar screen, but also the very idea of shopping for clothing is practically an exercise in torture for her! On the other hand, Sara will suspend whatever she is doing if there is an opportunity to go to the library or the bookstore. There are overflowing bookshelves lining every wall of her room, stacks of books on the floor, and books under the desk. The desk (barely visible to the naked eye) is adorned with a larger-than-life computer monitor, a miniature keyboard, and more books! There are horseshow ribbons hanging from the curtain rods and others covered in significant dust layers lying draped over the music stand. The laundry basket contains old, favorite stuffed animals—dragons, Pegasus, unicorns, and mythical creatures—while a growing pile of dirty laundry adorns the top of her dog's kennel. Occasional removal of the laundry pile will reveal her clarinet case. Sara knows where each favorite book is located and produces excellent college English essays from what mothers would call a dismal and utterly unkempt horror of a bedroom! This environment is to Sara "heavenly." It is where she spends most of her productive days and all of her peaceful nights. I have trained myself to remember Genesis 19 and what happened to Lot's wife. I don't look! Tarantulas the size of armadillos could be lurking in there, but I don't look!

Sara frequently had food stains on her sleeves and tangles in her hair, and I was often still questioning why God had chosen *me* as her mother. I was, however, taking comfort in knowing our child was completely "normal" in the flawless and unique way God created her. Being alone and being lonely were intertwined in her existence. Alone, she had found solace in her books (and self-directed discoveries) in contrast to the loneliness of not having *true* peers. Aloneness for Sara is like the satisfaction of food to a hungry man. We now felt empowered to end the loneliness she had endured by kicking open doors of access to her true peers—her "mental mates," as Dr. Palmer had explained. Our middle school trepidation had turned toward triumph with the increased understanding about the child God gave us. As Palmer said, "A primary need of most kids is to fit in." We've all heard terms like brain, nerd, geek, or worse applied to kids who seem too bookish or too 'into' school" (Palmer, 103). Sara was in fact endowed with a God-given academic potential, and we would now be able to more effectively advocate for her appropriate educational needs. We have come to realize just how much Sara is indeed "fearfully and wonderfully made" (Psalm 139:14 NASB).

FIVE

Professional Validation

Right on time, Dr. Palmer's written reports arrived in the mail. The information they contained was detailed, and with them, we fully understood just how rare a sparkling gem we had been entrusted with (which, quite frankly, further distressed my already unsettled nerves). We tucked the assessments safely in a drawer where they remained for about two months. My husband and I did not discuss them with anyone while we tried to process the information ourselves. As the start of seventh grade approached, I opened the drawer and, turning to the "Recommendations" section, read "work with your school team." We had solicited Dr. Palmer's advice for the purpose of taking it, though I had reservations our school district staff or teachers would be interested in being team players. My spouse was convinced, given our previous attempts to work with the school, that it would be a total waste of time. In our first meeting with district staff, my husband and I shared Dr. Palmer's findings with the superintendent of curriculum and requested an Individual Education Plan (IEP) that would help our daughter with her special needs for faster paced and more challenging curriculum. Copies of Dr. Palmer's assessments were given to the superintendent, and we were told we would have to meet another time with staff that handled both gifted assessments and individualized programs. At our second meeting, two officials informed us our request for an IEP could not be accommodated, "IEPs are only for students with medically diagnosed *disabilities*" and not for students who are able. Our child would have benefited from an Individual Education Plan designed to promote her maximum achievement toward her full potential. Clearly IEP is a misleading term and a service that was not accessible. We need programs (and administrators) in our schools that can operate with reasonable flexibility. We need officials who can build bridges of accommodation. Continuing in our team effort, we requested Sara's school day be reduced (two classes) to the state's minimum required hours. This was to allow Sara opportunity to attend one college course each semester in the daytime rather than late in the evening. Again, we needed another meeting to accommodate the school's principal, Sara's teachers, and the middle-school counselor to provide their input to that decision. The school year had begun when our third "team" meeting took place. Some parents hold to the idea that children should be seen and not heard (some teacher's classrooms are ordered this way too). I believed Sara's voice was paramount in decisions that would have major impact upon her life. She was present during the discussions when we suggested that college-level English (during the spring semester) and history (in the fall semester) could replace those grade-level subjects in our proposed reduction of school day hours. This idea was not well received by our other team members. The major area of teachers' concerns was "If Sara did not attend her grade-level classes, she would not be prepared to pass the seventh-grade standardized testing at the end of year." This thought was based on the college-level courses teaching different aspects of English and history. It was also more evidence of why I believe teachers are highly compelled to teach for the result of passing standardized test questions—even if our education officials say that is not the case. Our daughter had always scored well into the advanced levels of every standardized test she had ever taken, and we were not concerned that her current level of knowledge in these subjects would prevent her from passing the year-end exams for seventh grade. However, the teachers for those subjects were. Other concerns teachers brought to the table were Sara's seventh grade curriculum requirements, possible gaps in learning, the impact of hours of college homework on Sara's overall academic performance in middle school, and, of course, Sara's emotional well-being from missing socialization with her "peers." Some parents may have determined the course of their child's education path. We believed it was important to empower our daughter with her own voice and input. She had listened as the discussions took place and interjected her thoughts and opinions. At the end of our school team meeting, Sara was asked to express her opinion and thoughts. If Sara had determined she absolutely did not wish to remain in her middle school for the full day, my husband and I would certainly have pushed even harder for an alternative education accommodation. I was thinking of terms of "age discrimination" and wondering if it was time to enlist legal warriors at that point. Sara, however, through an emotionless voice and expressionless face, stated she would continue as usual with the six and a half hours of daily compulsory work. She explained, "I do my homework in class or at lunch anyway, so I'll still have time to go to college at night." Had she expressed anything else, my husband and I would have taken additional measures at that time. There is an old saying: "All things are bought at a price. The relevant issue is whether or not you are going to haggle over the payment." Potentially, Sara could have gained a two-hour reprieve from middle school that year, but the price would have been the negativity she would likely have experienced four and a half hours each day from her seventh grade instructors—potentially a high price to pay. No haggling came from Sara. Perhaps this was an incredible example of Sara's higher-level reasoning skills at work (or simply conflict avoidance).

Seventh grade began with no plan for individualized curriculum, no accommodation for a daytime higher-level challenge, and a status quo academic plan from our school "team." The school year progressed, and so too did Sara's misery. As the year went forward, Sara displayed a steadily increasing disgust in attending school. She was unwilling to produce grade-level assignments, finding them redundant and remedial. Teachers reported her failure to participate in classes. Her overall demeanor, scholastic enthusiasm, and GPA consistently fell. Completing repetitive assignments became a major area of contention. Other than science, where Sara was permitted to work on her own at a higher-level challenge, she displayed little interest in courses. Sara's methodology of meeting compulsory requirements was to wait until she had numerous missing assignments and a *D* grade on progress reports before going to her room and producing all missing assignments in short order, with little effort, and pulling her grades up to a *B* just in the nick of time. No discussion, discipline, or reward motived Sara to get compulsory assignments in on time. She had become completely apathetic. In her seventh grade English honors class, she spent the entire year reading books chosen from the state's recommended reading list for twelfth graders that she brought in from her personal collection. Completing the teacher's weekly book form that summarized student progress in reading was not a difficult task. Sara simply did not see the benefit or purpose of completing a form weekly, all year long, especially while she was independently reading five or six years beyond the grade level. She also did not agree with the requirement of making a replica of a religious artifact for a faith that was not her own in world history class. Why should she be required to make a decorated prayer rug representative of the Muslim faith while being prohibited from discussing anything related to Christianity? The birth of Christendom (Charlemagne in Rome 800), the Crusades (1095 in Jerusalem), and the Protestant Referendum (1517 in Germany) were not appropriate World History subject matters. The absolute authority endowed to the public school teachers was accepted by the majority of middle school students and their parents except the few like Sara and me. Sara wanted to discuss principles of fairness, justice, and equality within the instructors' lesson plans. Challenging the perceived absolute authority of our school officials, elected officials, or others is an area often difficult to quash in bright minds. Sara perceived some authority figures as obstinate, refusing to consider changing their determined course. No doubt some viewed Sara the same way. Sara was born with a propensity to seek answers. Her precocious nature drove her to question the *why* of many things. Sara responded to her squelched need for higher reasoning in a way she could—by consistently turning seventh grade assignments in late—no doubt out of spite and definitely in response to her frustration and anger! Not surprisingly, Sara had attended college at night and successfully passed a transferrable course, US History II—The Civil War Reconstruction to the Present. Sara had also passed a college-level, prerequisite English course. Undoubtedly her college-grade performance could have been increased if her classes had not been at night—and after many hours enduring boredom at compulsory grade level. Sara's college US History II professor commented, "Sara showed more academic focus than most of my students." This was consistent (as Dr. Palmer's assessment reports had explained) with Sara's sincere desire to learn higher-level course work, where she found the information intriguing and the class discussions more in line with her intellectual abilities. Whereas at her middle school Sara had put in the required physical attendance, endured material that moved at too slow a pace, and mentally wandered elsewhere, Sara had embraced the higher-level challenges her college night classes provided as evidence by the following term paper she submitted as a twelve-year-old in the fall of 2011.

The purpose of this paper is to answer the question, "Do you think that *The Paradox of American Power*, by Joseph S. Nye Jr., is relevant to Chapter 28 of the textbook, *Give Me Liberty: An American History; Volume Two*, by Eric Foner or does it "miss the mark" in relating to the textbook ?" This paper analyzes these two works looking for similarities and differences between the two. In examining the works, special attention has been paid to the textbook "Focus Questions" for Chapter 28. *The Paradox of American Power* is relevant to *Give Me Liberty: An American History, Volume Two,* and Chapter 28 because it shows situations worldwide that led to the events focused on in Chapter 28. They are similar because they both talk about War on Terrorism, George W. Bush, global warming and world governments. However, they differ in their emphasis.

A similarity between the two books is that they both address President Bush's handling of the events of 9-11. *Give Me Liberty*: Chapter 28 discusses the events of 9-11 and the next one hundred years. It focuses on the War on Terrorism; the role of President George W. Bush (before and after 9-11); confronting Iraq; other countries and the war; the economy, and long term consequences after 9-11. The chapter covers a lot of material, but it is really narrowly focused. The information is mainly about America's policies and decisions during Bush's second term as President. The chapter also gives information on President Bush's foreign policy. For example, Bush, acting for America, withdrew from the Anti-Ballistic Missile Treaty of 1972 and he "repudiated a treaty establishing an International Criminal Court" (1042).

In *The Paradox of American Power,* Nye talks about the establishment of a national security commission by President Bush following the 9-11 attacks. Nye also wrote that in 2001, a commission on national security had found, "America's military superiority would not protect us from hostile attacks on our homeland" (x). According to Nye, the terrorists were motivated by their religious fundamentalist beliefs and their hatred of American popular culture. American past times (movies, television) and values (freedom, individualism, feminism, open sexuality) given to Americans were reasons that terrorist's hatred grew. Nye also wrote that Iraq dislikes the United States (15). Foner agreed, giving reasons for Al Qaeda's hatred of America as: military bases in Saudi Arabia; American support for Israel; Anti-Islamic values; differences of religion; American views on sex; and American spending habits. Nye wrote that America was not listening to other countries and broke treaties and other agreements with them (xii).

Both selections globalized issues such as terrorism, global warming and world governments. In chapter 28 of *Give Me Liberty*, Foner wrote that President George W. Bush used American power to end existing treaties with other nations; remove environmental protections; and disregard global warming issues including the Kyoto Protocol on Climate Change. Other countries leaders and many Americans did not think highly of President Bush because of his unpopular use of influence and power. Foner noted, "To great controversy, the Bush administration announced that it would not abide by the Kyoto Protocol of 1997, which sought to combat global warming ... (1043)" And then, Nye stated, "President Bush had to reverse his early position that there was inadequate evidence of human effects on global warming" (83)

The *Paradox of American Power* discusses Globalization, and America's use of hard and soft power. This supplemental reading gives a wide view of American government, and global warming; global economy; even global public good. This book is really about America's relationship to the world and "global" policies like treaties. Military globalization, including humanitarian intervention and terrorism is included too. Sending our military to places like Somalia in Africa (to bring food to the starving) on a humanitarian mission is perceived as globally good. Also, sending our military as "peace keepers" to Bosnia or Kosovo during their war was globally good (87). Everyone seems to agree that doing things for the global public good is needed. Poor countries need assistance in developing so their economies can thrive; citizen health improve; and starvation become a thing of the past. George W. Bush said, "This is a great moral challenge" (146).

A more recent title is "social globalization." It is covered by the author and includes the "spread of peoples, cultures, images and ideas" (83). Globalization has entered "The Information Revolution" (41). An example of Information Revolution based social globalization is Facebook! But with The Information Revolution also came "hackers." Hackers have created and sent viruses around the world to attack software in computers globally. This has caused billions of dollars in damages to global economies. Social globalization sites make easy recruitment targets for terrorists. Terrorists have hacked into government computers (globally) and stolen information valuable to their employers and harmful to national security and safety. *The Paradox of American Power* briefly covers basics of 9-11 in the Preface but that is not the main purpose of the book. The author wrote that, "The tragedy on September 11, 2001, was a wake-up call for Americans" (ix). *The Paradox of American Power* tells the good, the bad, and the awful of America's "global" issues and discusses the effects of policies, soft and hard power influences, and political treaties and alliances. Global issues are the foundation of the book *The Paradox of American Power.*

Where the two texts differ is in the emphasis placed on different aspects of the War on Terror. Chapter 28 contains a lot of detail about 9-11. Chapter 28 starts with the attack on 9-11 and focuses heavily on Bush's "War on Terror" that followed. The reading material gives details about 9-11 including the planes captured by the hijackers. It also says, "Most of the dead were Americans, but citizens of over eighty other countries also lost their lives" (1039). It discusses how Al Qaeda was determined to be responsible for the attacks on innocent lives. The chapter explains why Al Qaeda would support the attacks on civilians going about their daily business on American soil. Also, the chapter describes the "thrusts of the war on terrorism" after the attacks as: spontaneous patriotism; sympathy for the victims; a rise in public trust for government; public servants became national heroes; common social purpose; and a shared traumatic experience (1043).

The Paradox of American Power talks about the lifestyle of Americans **before** September 11, 2001 and what steps Nye believes led up to the attacks. Nye claims Americans were disinterested in their countries foreign affairs and that they didn't care about Middle East politics or the rest of the world. Television networks programmed what the viewers wanted and closed foreign offices. They also "cut foreign news content by two-thirds" in order to program for the viewers' tastes. Nye claims most Americans were "focused on domestic affairs" and ignored the rest of the world. Basically, Nye wrote that Americans got lazy and didn't pay attention to what their government and other nations' governments were making decisions about; except for the few Americans who followed politics or global issues and were "arrogant" believing our country was "invincible and invulnerable" (ix).

In *The Paradox of American Power* contains the information and examples of hard and soft power; however details relating to the specific Chapter 28 in the textbook exist, but there are only a few. The textbook describes September 11, 2001 and the politics afterward with details. The supplemental reading supports the chapter, although limited to basic facts contained mainly in the Preface. It is not an accident that the target for the 9-11 attacks was directed at "financial firms housed in the World Trade Center" (1039) since America is powerful and wealthy or as Nye wrote, "[...] the United States is likely to remain the most powerful country well into this century [...]" (142).

Before, during, and after the 9-11 event many countries viewed America as arrogant and our President, George W. Bush, was perceived that way as well. We should remember what Nye reminds the reader of, that America "became complacent during the 1990's ... no country could match or balance us ..." and "Americans became arrogant about our power, arguing that we did not need to heed other nations" (ix). It is important for history not to repeat itself in another similar 9-11 event. The events of 9-11 also reminded American citizens that they are "one nation" even if they have different individual beliefs. Finally, *The Paradox of American Power* is relevant *to Give Me Liberty: An American History, Volume Two,* and Chapter 28 because it causes us to re-evaluate how the choices we made in the past affect the present and future (but it almost missed the mark)." (Hise 2008-2014)

The final academic irony of Sara's seventh grade year was that when the middle school offered a special field trip for students to tour a Los Angeles–area university campus, Sara was not permitted to attend, as space was limited and only eighth graders were going. I found it ludicrous that the only middle school–aged student in our entire county to have successfully passed an entire semester of college units was prevented from touring a university because she was *only* a seventh grader. This sealed my vote of no confidence in our school officials, and I held the opinion that they would be enthusiastic if we and our "different" child would simply forget our ideals and settle into the normal, conveyer belt– way things were handled in our national, state, county, and district schools. I also felt validated that I had discovered sound advice from many experts in giftedness who had provided me great insight in understanding our daughter's needs. "Once again, it falls to parents to advocate for their children's needs, often in the face of a hostile or indifferent educational system" (Solomon, "Would You Wish This On Your Child?", 53). Fortunately for my child, God gave me this advice: "Let us not lose heart when doing good, for in due time we will reap if we do not grow weary" (Galatians 6:9 NASB).

SIX

A Leap of Faith

We had consistently wanted to see Sara happy and enthusiast about learning. It was clear appropriate accommodations at middle school were not going to come. Our "team" efforts failed to generate accommodations more in line with Sara's abilities, resulting in the choking of her academic enthusiasm. Social isolation had become a six-hour-long daily experience. By its design, school is not a social venue, yet educators continually stress the importance of children socializing with their peers. Schools have established a schedule that limits student social time to lunch break but also separates student populations at lunchtimes. While the majority of our local educators consistently stated the importance of our daughter socializing with her age/grade peers, few were able to understand that those peers had already ostracized our daughter and sought friendships with others more like themselves. Thus, there was no socializing available, and these were *not* Sara's appropriate peers. Sara's nature was to protect herself from being singled out; that would only raise her feelings of difference. As early as third grade, her teacher had expressed, "Sara could easily have won her elementary school spelling bee but misspelled several words she clearly knew." Of course she did! Winners had to get up on stage and compete at district and potentially county competitions geared to recognize the "best." It made Sara happy *not* to have won! Had she deliberately dumbed down in order to avoid being recognized as "super smart" among her age peers and on a stage before a crowd? Sara had learned to self-identify as different through ongoing recognition of her high academic achievements. Recognition has the intention of being positive reinforcement. It had unfortunately backfired and resulted in unkind remarks or "bullying" from other age/grade-level pupils. Initially Sara had desired to be included and accepted by her peer group, but by virtue of her abilities, she had established a reputation that singled her out from that crowd.

After eight years of "accelerated learning," there was little hope acceptance would ever arrive from those same age/grade peers that education professionals persisted in channeling her toward. I have come to think that the daily disappointment in our educational system experienced by many youngsters might be greater than the stress of a death. Few people regularly discuss death with young students. Death is not continually in their faces, on their minds, or at their dinner tables. When a death occurs, a massive support network forms to emotionally assist youth—and that support forms in a nanosecond! Little (or no) support forms for the devastated or depressed student whose education dreams die. All students experience expectations to attain and maintain the best grades they possibly can, take coursework at challenging levels, maintain competitive scores on exams, look, act like and be accepted by classmates, and participate in extracurricular social activities with age/grade peers. Our

American students face these standardized expectations every day, and the majority have adapted to this stress. The traditional student has true peers in the classroom and on the campus to share his or her concerns and lend the student support. There are also built in support systems in the forms of subject clubs, after-school tutoring, and study groups. What if the student *is* truly "different?" What if he or she can't conform to "normal" and will never "fit in?" Where is the support network for the frustrated nonconformist? It is generally nonexistent! What we experienced was the traditional educational matrix—every child had better be on it, moving at the correct pace, no speedy deviants permitted! Our inflexible educational system threatened to topple our "deviant" student who was once enthusiastic. It frustrated us beyond measure!

Our motivation for advanced learning opportunities has never been one pushed forward by the potential glory of saying, "Look at what Sara has done!" Any parental boasting or public spotlight on our young child's abilities would have been a great disservice to her. I had mentioned to Dr. Palmer our repeatedly being told by school teachers and district staff the importance of peer socialization. I asked if we should be concerned. "Who are her peers—her chronological age group or her mental mates?" he replied. "Eventually, we all become adults." I loved this response because it gave me peace of mind then, and has every day since. It also gave me a sense of direction on where to place our energies when seeking to meet our daughter's individual needs. Sara did not have mental mates to socialize with in her seventh grade environment. She was reading *The Immortal Life of Henrietta Lacks* at age twelve and discovering the impact that culturing human HELA cells for medical science research has had worldwide (Skloot 2010). Sara was processing the racial and other injustices contained in this nonfiction biography and had no mental mates in middle school to discuss it with. Sara's needs were to obtain her appropriate level of education and to socialize with those who could discuss more advanced subject materials with her. As Dr. Palmer had explained, Sara has a need for "higher level of reasoning," even if she is chronologically a child. Not unlike other profoundly gifted students, Sara also had limited alternate education resources, advisors, and opportunities to develop at her natural rate and abilities.

I would not be inclined to say that the current education system does not work for anyone. It just doesn't work for everyone. It certainly was not working for our member of the top one percent of the general population. The middle school team results we had hoped for had not been fruitful. Our daughter was still stuck on the perpetual conveyer belt of a system that was not in her favor. A system developed for age/grade-level education that was performance focused and was operating just as it had always done. Sara's compulsory-level performance and her self-esteem were at all-time lows. She was increasingly depressed about hours spent in classrooms, forced to listen to information she had already mastered. She repeatedly complained of teachers giving out lengthy instructions she did not require, often for assignments in areas she had surpassed or already completed independently. Repetitive daily homework assignments, rote and unnecessary, were exercises in tedious boredom. Her attentiveness was absent. Teachers disciplined Sara for wanton disengagement, complaining Sara had "checked out" and begun to "doodle" on every piece of paper and even on her erasers. Meanwhile, Sara was still passing night courses at the college. I know some wonderful teachers and staff in our local district who have loved Sara over the years and would have been willing to meet her needs at her academic level were it not for restrictive policies. I am not proposing we abolish the education system that generally works for the majority (though some in my local school district may think I should be permanently blacklisted from anything education related). It is my intention to share with other parents, *not only* the parents of accelerated learners, why they also might need to take a different approach to fulfilling their children's academic needs. I think it is important for school boards, district administrators, staff, teachers, and counselors to truly listen with open minds when parents plead for accommodations. I am not suggesting that parents push school district boundaries when their student has *not* been well documented for accommodations in specific areas, advanced or otherwise. Having solicited professional advice, referring to recommendations, referencing solid research, and investigating additional source materials, my husband and I had attempted to work within the constraints of a ridged system. Working as a team with our child's school officials had failed. Flexibility was stifled.

I wanted to be careful with the authority God had given me to make decisions for Sara. I researched every "gifted" thing I could think of. It must have appeared to my husband that I spent some of his entire workdays in our home sitting at my computer. I had discovered much. Magnet schools in urban areas have opportunities for like-minded intellectuals to group together in their academic courses. We had no magnet school in our district. Beyond fifth grade, Sara had no local access or education venue bringing her true peers together. Great programs did and do exist—outside our area. We would have loved to enroll our daughter in opportunities suggested by Dr. Palmer, such as Stanford University's EPGY program. Unfortunately it was only during the summer, was beyond our financial means, and would not have addressed Sara's daily need for challenge and a faster-paced learning. Stanford's online high school program would have been a great option, but it would not have given Sara access to socialize with people face to face and would have required Sara to complete each compulsory grade (although at her own pace). Johns Hopkins University has a program called Talent Search, and Johns Hopkins also offers wonderful learning opportunities Sara had qualified for. It too was offered only in the summer at its main campus in Baltimore, Maryland, the other side of the contiguous United States. Johns Hopkins was also even farther out of our financial reach. University of Nevada at Reno, which partners with the Davidson Institute, offers a daytime school enrollment for gifted students. It is necessary for at least one parent to live in the Reno area. Organized meetings with youth of various ages enrolled in American Mensa (which Sara is) were occasionally held in Orange County, California. Unfortunately the drive distance precluded our daughter from participating. Homeschooling was an option but not the *best option* for our daughter since she would spend a majority of time working independently and perhaps continue to view herself as a "lone freak." It may seem that I have made excuses for every option that was available. I could not accept that in order to *appropriately* educate our child, my spouse would need to leave his current employment and find someone to fill his position as primary caregiver for his elderly parent, and that we would need to relocate to an urban area. Our alternative was to maintain two separate households great distances apart while maintaining a long-distance marriage. This option would have at times made Sara a latchkey kid, a child left alone while I worked to support our second household and still maintained my availability to drive her to classes at a commuter-only school. Relocating out of the area or consistently traveling long distances were options we had taken off the table. They simply were not reasonable options.

Sara's needs were significant, but we had other children who also needed their parents. The recent American economic crisis followed by the economic downturn had continued over the fiscal cliff. This had sent one adult son on the road to higher education (because of few job openings and discontinued unemployment income). He moved home and into our travel trailer located in our driveway. Our eldest daughter was pursuing her education at the university level with Parent Plus loans, increasing our debt-to-income ratio. Another son was planning his East Coast wedding, and he wanted all his family members to attend and his siblings to participate as members of his wedding party. Did I forget to mention the groom's parents traditionally pay for the rehearsal dinner? We had an array of needs to meet in addition to those required by Sara. Our minor child who was still at home and her education were paramount but not our sole focus. I was passionate about obtaining the appropriate education for Sara. That education, however, which would initiate face-to-face contact and conversations discussing the same level of shared knowledge or shared interests, eluded us because of Sara's age. It seemed reasonable that such an education should be available within our local area. My unfaltering commitment was to secure for Sara the best learning environment for the unique individual she is. I was not willing to settle for less than a well-adjusted, emotionally secure, and academically thriving daughter. Sara should have felt proud to embrace her unique attributes as fabulous characteristics and not as "freakish" or disturbing traits to be ashamed of. Yet she had a growing tendency to shut herself up within the safe walls of her bedroom. I had become even more proactive in pushing for Sara's access to greater learning opportunities. Sporadic enrichment programs were not as suitable as consistent involvement. It was not a competitive race to see if Sara could get to a higher level education in less time than another student. Rather it was a race to maintain a healthy, active mind and avoid it sinking into a dark and depressing isolation. We continued our commitment to meeting Sara's special needs for the academic education most appropriate for her. Although some competitive parents or competitive children sound the alarm "advance, advance, advance, and never retreat," that was *not* our motto! Our daughter's happiness had consistently been our focus and something that receiving an appropriate education would generate. That necessary education, significantly more challenging and given at a faster pace, was available, but

Sara's access to it had been continually restricted. We had numerous conversations with Sara about what she thought her ideal situation would be. She wanted to go to the community college in the daytime and take whatever she wanted to learn. That seemed a reasonable desire coming from our twelve-year-old. For three years she had been taking evening classes, not online but on the campus, and had completed a full semester of transferrable units in foreign language, history, and English. She had informed us that she "likes it there because no one treats me different. If they did, they'd treat me like I was a kid, but they don't—I'm just normal there." When the conversation turned to her enrollment at her middle school, she asked, "Why do they want me to be bored when all I want to do is learn?" There is the answer to the ultimate question. "When is radical acceleration the best option for a child?" Everything I had read in books, all my online research, and all the questions I'd asked people whom I trusted could not have given me a better answer. Every child is unique, and his or her circumstances and needs are just as individual as he or she is. Sara's need was to learn *and* to do it where she "was just normal." Dr. Palmer had written, "As a school psychologist, one of the main criteria I use when placing children in any special program is their comfort level with being there … Most children have a good sense of what they need and where they belong" (Palmer, 49). He had also written (subsection, "What's Your Gut Feeling?"), "Once you have gathered all the information you can … get back in tune with your instincts – your parent radar … Go with that instinct, and remember your decision doesn't have to be permanent" (Palmer, 50). Full-time college at twelve was not unheard of; it was just very rarely heard of. Sara's enthusiasm and eagerness to make the radical jump was tempered by the lack of support I felt we had in taking such an unusual course. Questions, even those asked in fervent prayer, often lead us to other questions.

- Was radical acceleration the only avenue we could take?
- Were we fully prepared to advocate for Sara's radical acceleration, and was the time for impulsion now?
- Had I garnered enough educated opinions on the pros and cons of acceleration?
- Was I armed with all the documentation necessary to acquire for our daughter the appropriate level of education she both deserved and desired?
- Had I consulted with others more knowledgeable, and was I confident Sara's current and future emotional needs would also be served?
- Was I confident Sara had the maturity to engage in all subject courses at the college level and to obtain passing grades in them?

After careful consideration and fervent prayer, we eventually got off our prayerful knees and took a leap of faith. The most informed educational decision was made. Sending our very young minor child into an adult learning environment as a full-time day student had not been our initial goal—it had become our only option. We would radically accelerate Sara, and she would skip the remaining five compulsory grades of public education. I don't know who originally said it, or I would certainly give credit where credit is due, but we make decisions with the information we have available at the time. If we receive more, or different, information later on it does not mean we made a poor decision—it means we made the best decision we could with the information we had available. Knowing our decision didn't have to be permanent was comforting. But knowing we had trusted Sara to express to us where she felt a sense of belonging, where she was happy, and where she had expressed committed interest in an environment that was conducive to her attaining knowledge—that made me feel fantastic! No doubt there are other exceptional minds in our public schools. Some may miss opportunities to expand and thereby delay or fail to reach their full potential. Perhaps later in life those exceptional minds will find a new spark to reignite an interest and jump back onto their course. Sara was not interested in a five-year holding pattern that would lead to high school dating, powder puff football, drama club activities, and prom night, as they were little reason to continue subjecting herself to ongoing years of frustration with stunted academic growth. I had learned that behind each secured door of opportunity was another—usually one that has also had a deadbolt to remove. Sara knew what was working for her, where she felt good emotionally and fulfilled intellectually. Confident in our understanding of Sara's emotional, social, and academic needs, her father and I determined to radically accelerate in order to curb Sara's waning self-image and secure higher-level academic challenges for her.

Many gifted children choose between being ostracized and going underground; many disidentify, attempting to seem less accomplished for the sake of peer approval. One survey of super-high-IQ students showed that four out of five were constantly monitoring themselves in an attempt to conform to the norms of less gifted children; in another study, 90 percent were unwilling to be identified as part of the "brain" crowd. ... In the 1990's Miraca Gross studied children who were radically accelerated, starting college between eleven and sixteen. None regretted the acceleration, and most had made good and lasting friendships with older children. (Solomon, Far from the Tree, 458)

At times our decisions have exposed me to strong viewpoints against our chosen route; it also exposed me to strong supporters of it. I would be the first to admit that navigating this unusual path has been controversial. Sara was setting a precedent in our small community and I often wondered if the staff and instructors would be unbiased and fair. I couldn't help wondering if there was a true willingness to accommodate Sara's special need, or simply a reluctant accommodation through a legal loophole I had inadvertently discovered and pursued. By far, my strongest supporter has said, "I will instruct you and teach you in the way which you should go; I will counsel you with My eye upon you." (Psalm 32:8 NASB)

Sara's first full-time college semester she and I both felt weighed down by a lurking heaviness. It felt as though everyone associated with our local educational institutions (former teachers, K-12 administrators, college officials) was speculating on whether twelve year old Sara would indeed be able to handle the full-time challenges of college level coursework. When final grades were posted for the fall term of 2012 Sara's semester GPA (carrying 14 units and factoring in her earlier concurrent semesters) was permanent at 3.21 on a 4.0 scale. We exhaled. The feeling she had been delicately walking on glass shards under a public spot light had finally ended for Sara. The next three semesters were delightfully fun and adventurous for her. She sailed through interesting subjects that challenged her mind and provoked her to consider the possibilities of her future. She was at ease with fellow students and her academic performance met requirements of her instructors. I did not read the article "Are We Failing Our Geniuses?" in Time Magazine until years after its publication but the sentiments expressed are the exact route we choose to follow with Sara.

> Ideally, school systems should strive to keep their most talented students through a combination of grade skipping and other approaches (dual enrollment in community colleges, telescoping classwork without grade skipping) ... The best way ... is to let them grow up in their own communities–by allowing them to skip ahead at their own pace. (Cloud, 46)

I only wish I had been reading *Time* magazine in 2007 when our daughter was much younger and prior to the many barriers to this ideal that we have faced. I would not have delayed so long in pursuing radical acceleration to meet Sara's special needs. Sara described her experience following her admission as a special full-time enrollment student at her local community college this way, "I feel like the person Robert Frost wrote about in his famous poem." He said,

> Two roads diverged in a wood and I—
> I took the one less traveled by,
> And that has made all the difference (Untermeyer 2002).

What makes this statement insightful is that Robert Frost did not say that the road taken was obviously perfect, or without a doubt smoother. In fact, his poem describes that both paths appeared equally as nice. The author eloquently wrote a poem explaining that when one comes to a divide a choice has to made (unless one intends to remain immobile at the fork in the road forever). In Sara's case, one road led to another year at middle school followed by four years in high school. Sara had seen her sister prepare for and participate in high school coursework, Homecoming dances, and Prom night activities. She had been to local high school football games where her sister had been a member in the marching band. Her brother had been in his high school drama club. Sara had attended both middle school and high school graduations of her siblings with all their pomp and circumstance. Sara did not have a desire to take that road. She had no interest delaying her voracious appetite for the rigors of academic challenges to participate in less strenuous course work, or to participate in the social or extracurricular activities her siblings had enjoyed. The other road led to full-time student status at the community college level. Sara did have personal experience with the homework load, the adult learning environment, and the level of academic challenges college courses entailed. Cerro Coso Community College had no precedent for accepting a full time pupil as young as Sara. Without a doubt this was the road less traveled and time has proven it to have been the better path for Sara. I believe parents considering a radical acceleration (skipping more than one or two grades) should attempt to achieve accommodations with their school officials and teachers first, just as Dr. Palmer had suggested. In a perfect education system, each "different" learner would be supported by educators and parents alike. Educators holding vigorously to the way things have always been structured is not beneficial in reaching amicable alternatives for the success of our "different" students. Student success is also not advanced by zealous parents whose motivation is self-serving.

Sara is the child God chose to give us. Among her recognitions for her academic accomplishments is the highest academic honor (given to elementary school students). The United States President's Award for Outstanding Academic Excellence was presented to Sara as she prepared to leave her elementary school. Sara's certificate was accompanied by a letter signed by our nation's forty-fourth president, Barack Obama. On March 17, 2010, President Obama wrote,

> This honor is a testament to your determination and commitment to excellence ... Nothing is more important to our Nation's long-term success than preparing our future leaders for the world they will inherit. We face great challenges as a country, and we will need young people like you to take up these

challenges and make them your own. As you step into the current of history, I encourage you to cultivate a love of learning, serve your community, and reach for your highest aspirations. (Obama 2010)

Thirty-nine years *earlier,* Paul D. Plowman had provided this insight, specific to gifted children, in a report to California's Department of Education:

There is growing recognition of the need for federal leadership and financial support for educational programs that will develop the intellectual and creative potential of children, youth, and adults. This is needed if we are to solve the horrendous social, economic, and political problems that confront this State and Nation. (Plowman, 16)

President Obama's encouragement is an impressive letter, and the honor of the recognition is certainly appreciated by our daughter. Developing and funding a federal gifted education program for advanced and accelerated learners "with intellectual and creative potential" would be more beneficial to our nation's future, than instructing those youth to reach for "highest aspirations" that are not available or affordable to them. Available academic challenges and financial support would go far in assisting Sara, and other gifted students, to "cultivate learning, serve their communities and reach their aspirations." Individuals with attributes such as Sara's should indeed be supported in the hopes that one day they might be able, as Plowman reported, "to solve the horrendous social, economic, and political problems that confront this State and Nation." It appears preparing this population of youth to solve horrendous issues is a lofty ideal left over from 1971, and a population our esteemed legislators have chosen *not* to endorse with financial support.

Advocating for Sara has been challenging. I am the mother God chose for her, "For you created my inmost being; you knit me together in my mother's womb" (Psalm 139:13 NIV). It has become clearer to me just why God has paired the two of us. I am often bold and determined. Sara needed a bold, determined, and fearless mother to advocate for her needs and for her right to an appropriate education. Sometimes my horses (animals weighing over one thousand pounds and known for unpredictable actions) have indeed found me fearless. Certainly some educators do now! I have been called difficult, obstinate, and even misguided while advocating for what I believed were Sara's best interests, those of her guaranteed legal right to a "free and *appropriate* education." Some people have persisted in their viewpoints that my husband and I were leaping with our child over a radically accelerated cliff. Indeed! We were leaping—into a fruitful environment of advanced opportunities! I have not been disappointed with the benefits that have subsequently become available to the child God gave me. It has not always been easy for me to draw strength from Scripture. In fact, it has often been a challenge to remember I have never been alone, "Is not your fear *of God* your confidence, And the integrity of your ways your hope?" (Job 4:6 NASB)

Photo Credit: Jenny Hazlewood

SEVEN

Legal Issues to Consider

Each parent, wherever he or she is, should find the path that is correct for his or her child. Seeking those opportunities that fit each individual child's needs may require investigating legislation your state may have in existence. We know beyond any doubt that Sara's path was correct for Sara. My own personal relationship with Google led me to California Assembly Bill 2207 (sponsored by Baldwin). AB2207 was chaptered (1073) into the California Education Code in May of 2000. No one told me of this legal right and opportunity that was available to Sara and others like her. I discovered it on my own while performing my own research. Here is an excerpt from Assembly Bill 2207.

THE PEOPLE OF THE STATE OF CALIFORNIA DO ENACT AS FOLLOWS:

SECTION 1. (a) The Legislature finds and declares all of the following:

(1) Highly gifted and talented pupils, those whose measured intelligence quotient is 150 or more points,

possess enormous potential for intellectual attainment, personal achievement, and social contribution.

(2) Because highly gifted and talented pupils are often assigned to elementary and secondary schools that are not equipped to offer them an appropriate education, their full potential may not be developed and they may experience an unsatisfactory adjustment to school that may cause them to lose interest, drop out, or even contemplate or commit suicide.

(3) The intelligence level of highly gifted and talented pupils obscures the fact that they are a special population with special needs.

(b) It is, therefore, the intent of the Legislature to enact legislation to ensure that all pupils, including highly gifted and talented pupils, receive a free and appropriate education. It is further the intent of the Legislature to enact legislation to increase the options available for providing services to highly gifted and talented pupils including an opportunity for highly gifted and talented pupils to attend classes in the public postsecondary institutions of this state. (C. D. Education n.d.)

Discovering this legislation does not mean we simply transferred Sara from our local middle school into our local community college. For most things, especially those involving law, there is always a process. Legal processes generally take time and patience. This route also took dedication, follow up, and follow through. Radical acceleration of children into an adult learning environment requires parents to understand that their child will be treated as any other college student would be. There are no special considerations at the college level just because your minor is a student on campus. Before other parents or students jump on board with enthusiasm, I believe they should consider some long-term aspects of this route. Sara did not graduate from eighth or twelfth grades—she never attended eighth through twelfth grades! AB2207 students do not automatically receive a high school diploma. The California Department of Education exempts these students; it does not automatically graduate them. Students and parents considering this route may find it a disadvantage or a diploma they are not willing to sacrifice. Students under AB2207 may be able to apply to take the California High School Proficiency Examination (CHSPE), which is California's only legal equivalent of a high school diploma. There are requirements you will want to investigate, such as age and compulsory grade level completion. With radical acceleration students could potentially have obtained an associate degree from a California community college or even a bachelor's degree from a four-year institution prior to taking the CHSPE. Getting a high school diploma at that point is rather a redundant prospect in my opinion. If a high school diploma is important to you or to your student, AB2207 is probably not the route for you.

When bright young minds stay the course of traditional age/grade education, they have the opportunity to achieve higher grade-point averages (GPAs). It stands to reason, with less strenuous curriculum than college-level coursework, students would have an easier time hitting the higher marks. Traditional students also have the potential to obtain many scholarship opportunities for colleges due to their exceptionally high (grade-level) GPAs. Radical acceleration under AB2207 removes many scholarship opportunities as well as many four-year colleges from availability. High school students with good study habits and a strong desire to learn have advanced placement (AP) courses available. AP courses are an opportunity for high school students to take more strenuous high school subjects (culminating in an examination that students must pass) for college credit. Many high school students have saved thousands of dollars on future college expenses by taking several or more AP courses over the years of their high school education. High grade-point averages and passing advanced placement courses equal scholarship opportunities and college-cost savings. Money often talks. The benefit of AB2207 is that it allows bright young students to enter higher-level curriculum challenges and to soar toward those heights of learning at paces they are capable of. It does not hold students back who have already forged ahead independently. Their grades in such difficult coursework may not be the As the student was easily achieving in his or her age/grade enrollment. When applying for future scholarships to universities as a transfer student, college GPAs may be lower than if the student had stayed the course through traditional K–12 education and applied directly to a university. In this sense, radical acceleration could have a negative effect on a student's entrance into four-year schools due to a lower GPA attained during community-college course work. Also, scholarships for four-year institutions as a transfer student from a community college may be fewer and farther between than those for students entering four-year institutions directly from high school. This has been our experience. The radically accelerated student who goes farther and sooner in his or her education has not been awarded a lifetime free pass through academia. Many scholarship opportunities exist for K–12 students (some specific to gifted students). Most, if not all, have qualification requirements that restrict applications to students in a specific grade level or within a particular age range. Sara has been disqualified by both of these criteria. Many opportunities for funding Sara's continued academic achievements have been removed by our decision to radically accelerate her. There will be no savings from high school AP courses. We can expect to pay for every upper-division course our student takes in ongoing educational pursuits. I advise parents to spend significant amounts of time searching scholarship and grant opportunities but to be prepared to pay all expenses out of pocket for accelerated education (beyond a California community college acceptance under AB2207). Again, money often talks when determining the course for your child's education. Scholarship qualifications on nearly all we have investigated, including those through 4-H, have required attainment of ages seventeen or eighteen, grade-point averages of 3.5–4.0, specific ethnicities, specific career-field majors, or parents with poverty-level income status. For the very young and very bright mind that radically soars ahead of his or her age/grade peers, educational aid is virtually non-existent.

Finally, parents should keep in mind that many of our four-year institutions do not accept early-entrance transfer students. In fact, most I checked on do not! The reasoning is based on the liability of housing such young students in dormitories with their general adult populations. And would you really want your youngster in a coed dorm room with young adults? Many people have assumed institutions of higher learning would be recruiting bright and willing young minds like Sara's. Truly, there are very few institutions willing to take such a risk. When compared to the students who have completed the traditional compulsory route (who are or soon will be adults), opportunities for accelerated minors (those who skipped grades) are scarce. Barriers, however well intentioned, often restrict admission of the very students who would thrive and soar if allowed to soak up the knowledge that is inaccessible to them. Parents need a long-term plan if their children will still be minors when they are ready to enter university-level courses. If scholarship opportunities are important to you as a parent or entrance into a specific university or four-year school is on your child's heart, legislation such as AB2207 is probably not the route for you. On the other hand, if your student is like ours—miserable in his or her current environment, yearning for something greater, proven in his or her abilities, comfortable with going alone onto a campus full of adult learners, or sliding into depression—then you should read the entire written document of the California legislature's Assembly Bill 2007. Those in other states will have to research legislation that may exist in their own states of residency. Only you and your child can ascertain the correct path for your student. AB2207 was the correct educational choice for Sara, but that does not mean it is the correct path for all gifted students. The process that we adhered to in order to gain the appropriate education we sought for our daughter is printed below.

SEC. 3. Section 48800.5 of the Education Code is amended to read:

48800.5. (a) A parent or guardian of any pupil, regardless of the pupil's age or class level, may petition the governing board of the school district in which the pupil is enrolled to authorize the attendance of the pupil at a community college as a special full-time student on the ground that the pupil would benefit from advanced scholastic or vocational work that would thereby be available. If the governing board denies the petition, the pupil's parent or guardian may file an appeal with the county board of education, which shall render a final decision on the petition in writing within 30 days.

(b) If the governing board denies a request for a special full-time enrollment at a community college for a pupil who is identified as highly gifted, the board shall issue its written recommendation and the reasons for the denial within 60 days. The written recommendation and denial shall be issued at the next regularly scheduled board meeting that falls at least 30 days after the request has been submitted.

(c) Any pupil who attends a community college as a special full-time student pursuant to this section is exempt from compulsory school attendance under Chapter 2 (commencing with Section 46100) of Part 26. (C. D. Education n.d.)

Adhering to the above requirements, my husband and I prepared the necessary documents on Sara's behalf and submitted them to the proper authorities at the completion of Sara's miserable seventh grade school year.

This is a petition, in accordance to Educational Code Section 48800.5, to authorize student (Sara Hise) to attend "community college as a special full-time student on the ground that the pupil would benefit from advanced scholastic or vocational work that would thereby be available" EC 48800.5 (a).

We the parents of Sara feel that her unique education needs are not currently being met by the programs offered through SSUSD and that we have made the appropriate attempts to call attention to Sara's specially gifted abilities and to work with SSUSD to develop a plan which would ensure that Sara's abilities were being matched academically. However at this point SSUSD has not taken satisfactory action and that SSUSD has therefore not met the intent of EC 48800.5, or the Assembly Bill AB 2207 which, in amending EC 48800 and 48800.5 in 2000, legally defines Sara in the category of "highly gifted and talented," as such (emphasis ours):

SECTION 1. (a) The Legislature finds and declares all of the following:

(1) Highly gifted and talented pupils, those whose measured intelligence quotient is 150 or more points, possess enormous potential for intellectual attainment, personal achievement, and social contribution.

(2) Because highly gifted and talented pupils are often assigned to elementary and secondary schools that are not equipped to offer them an appropriate education, **their full potential may not be developed and they may experience an unsatisfactory adjustment to school that may cause them to lose interest, drop out**, or even contemplate or commit suicide.

(3) The intelligence level of highly gifted and talented pupils obscures the fact that they are a **special population with special needs**.

(b) It is, therefore, the intent of the Legislature to enact legislation to ensure that all pupils, including highly gifted and talented pupils, receive a free and appropriate education. It is further the intent of the Legislature to enact legislation to increase the options available for providing services to highly gifted and talented pupils including an **opportunity for highly gifted and talented pupils to attend classes in the public postsecondary institutions of this state.**

What SSUSD has, in concert with Cerro Coso Community College (CCCC), is only *concurrent enrollment,* which is far from what the Educational Code would provide for Sara if faithfully acted upon by SSUSD. As such, the policies adopted by SSUSD and CCCC have worked against Sara's ability by limiting her options as to how she might meet her own level of need for academic challenge, and to which she is entitled under California Educational Code law.

- Concurrent students are prohibited from registering until "regular" college students have enrolled and are prohibited from "wait listing" courses.
- Concurrent students are limited to evening and/or night courses available after completing compulsory hours of attendance at grade level in secondary schools.
- The limited number of available evening courses often require late night labs and thereby are inappropriate for a student required at early morning compulsory classes.
- Sara has successfully completed 12 semester units of postsecondary work (beginning postsecondary work at age nine years) and desires to continue in the challenging curriculum which would be available to her during daytime hours.
- Sara has been thoroughly evaluated by a licensed Educational Psychologist specializing in giftedness.
- Sara has specific needs related to her level of giftedness which would be met as a day student attending community college.

- The student meets the criteria listed by California law under AB2207 Sec 4, EC Section 52201(b).
- The student has successfully passed the same college level entrance examination required of graduating high school seniors as administered by CCCC staff.

Sara has previously been deemed ineligible for an Individualized Educational Plan (IEP) by SSUSD as she does not meet policy criteria, e.g. "disability." Restricted access to college courses as a "concurrent student" has twice resulted in her inability to enroll in coursework for which she is intellectually suited. Such restrictions are eliminated under AB2207. In addition, Sara has been marked "absent" for classes she's missed while attending college level courses by SSUSD teachers; an almost retaliatory response from SSUSD with regard to her meeting her own unique and demonstrated education needs which are currently beyond the level provided by SSUSD.

Under section 48800.5 of the above education code, approving this petition would provide this student with a program of study in accordance with Sara's profoundly gifted needs and the provision of law. Sara's IQ score places her between 99.5[th] and 99.9[th] percentile above the general population. AB2207 specifically targets students such as Sara Hise with protections and provisions addressing the academic and emotional needs of highly gifted students.

While we recognize that there are areas of learning in which our student has not been exposed and therefore has not yet mastered, her unusual abilities warrant her placement among her intellectual peers. We have met numerous times with SSUSD and CCCC educators and officials during previous years. We have solicited the professional advice of experts in giftedness. After considerable thought, and patience with trying to work within the programs provided by SSUSD, we now petition that Sara be allowed to attend CCCC as a full-time student, according to EC 48800.5(b)

48800.5 (b) A pupil who attends a community college as a special full-time student pursuant to this section is exempt from compulsory school attendance under Chapter 2 (commencing with Section 46100) of Part 26.

We appreciate your consideration to this issue. Documents supporting this petition are enclosed.

Sincerely,
Kevin and Tamara Hise

encl. (2) Assessment
             Transcript

Our local school district had never encountered this situation prior to our petition. After receiving it, the district superintendent first required the middle school principal to submit a recommendation based upon her opinion and interactions with our daughter. A copy of this recommendation was never provided to us nor was it included in the copies of our student's cumulative file we requested from the district offices years later. We were informed verbally that the principal's opinion was "favorable" and had recommended our student's petition be approved. The district superintendent's office informed us they too had given their approval. However, final approval from our local elected school board members was required. We were told our petition pertained to a minor child where backup documents including those from Sara's school cumulative file contained confidential information (an area of protection) under the Brown Act; therefore, members of the school board met in closed session. We were not privy to their discussion and no minutes are taken during closed sessions per the rules of the Brown Act. Following the meeting and at my request, we received a document on school district letterhead acknowledging our specifically named child had been legally exempted from further compulsory education, August 1, 2012, by school board vote of six "ayes," with "noes" totaling one. The exemption did not mean that our student was permitted to register for a full load of college coursework, uninhibited and unconstrained. In actuality, it meant we advanced to step two of a legal process. We were then able to petition for enrollment into any of California's 112 community colleges, *each* of which under "self-governance" had the authority to approve or deny our request for admission.

Our local community-college district, with three colleges, each with main campuses and satellite locations, has an average annual enrollment of twenty-six thousand students. Our community-college district had also never experienced this situation. The K-12 superintendent's office had contacted our local community-college vice president of student services directly when their office had received our petition for exemption from K–12 and throughout the K–12 school district's processing of it. The receipt of our later petition for Sara's admission to college under AB2207 was no surprise to the local college. The year prior, I had notified the vice

119

president of student services of the college that this might be a route we would have to take in the future. Our petition for admission was submitted with a copy of our exemption from the K–12 district, and we began the second stage of AB 2207's (ED 48800.5) process. Establishing communication rather than embracing secrecy had alleviated some drag on this second half of the AB2207 process. However, as a precedent was being set, no one knew exactly the steps to take in order to accommodate a minor who was no longer a "concurrently enrolled" student. The president of Cerro Coso Community College had initially stated the college did not have authority to approve our petition. The petition was passed to the chancellor of Kern Community College District, who determined it was a matter for the full Kern Community College District's Board of Trustees. However, the board would not meet on the issue until after the deadline for enrollment had passed, so our petition reverted to the chancellor. In the meantime, the district's general counsel gave a ruling that the college was not authorized to "waive" fees as they do for K–12 concurrent enrollment pupils. This caused me to confront the vice president of student services with the actual wording of the legislation, "entitled to free and appropriate," as well as pointing out the state's legislature had established provision in the state's Mandates Claim Fund ($1,000,000.00) for costs incurred by community colleges relating to AB2207. If not tuition and processing fees, what other "costs" could my child cause her local community college to incur? This discussion prompted the vice president of student affairs to send the ruling back to the college district's general counsel for clarification. In the meantime and under time constraints, the chancellor had approved Sara's admission with the petition to go on the Board of Trustees' next agenda as an "informational item." The office of the Cerro Coso Community College President then issued a letter (September 16, 2012) stating Sara had been admitted as a special full time enrollment student "based on the process set forth by Education Code 48800.5."

Having taken required subject-placement tests (just as any high school graduate is required to do), our daughter enrolled as a full-time student taking English composition, Latin I, US History I and a fine art. It had often been difficult to remember that the God of Joshua was also looking after Sara now in our modern time. However, His evidence was clear. The Lord had planned for Joshua to win his battle. "See, I have given Jericho into your hand, with its king *and* the valiant warriors" (Joshua 6:2 NASB). I do feel the battle with district policies, district lawyers, and educators with strong opinions has definite similarities to Jericho—such as our walking round and round the walls of institutions of learning, trying to gain access to appropriate levels of education! God was indeed accomplishing the plan He has always had for Sara (and providing the desires of Sara's heart). "A man's heart plans his way, But the LORD DIRECTS HIS STEPS" (Proverbs 16:9 NKJV).

Photo Credit: Tammy Thoms

EIGHT

Jumping with Confidence

Sara has been faithful, courageous, and determined to acquire the level of education she has been capable of. She has consistently obtained high marks in all college coursework. Although not Sara's main goal and contrary to her private nature and personality, she has earned many recognition and commendation certificates from members of the United States Congress, senators, and from California's State Assembly. A sitting United States president has encouraged Sara to proceed in her educational journey for the benefit of her nation's future. That journey is fast advancing toward its next challenge level. What doors will open so that Sara can in fact "reach for her highest aspirations" as President Obama's letter encouraged her to do. Access denied will send Sara into "the current of history" where she would continue to be prevented or delayed from advancing toward her four-year degree and beyond. It has been a struggle to work against a rigid system that for over fifty years has lessened its willingness to meet the known and legally documented special needs of exceptional students. We have the capacity to provide for all of our students the best learning opportunities to address Plowman's prediction come true, "the horrendous national problems" they've inherited. We cannot expect our next generation of patriots to address, impact, and work out the problems inherited from previous generations unless we provide them all the tools for success that they will require. Radical acceleration has provided Sara access to the tools of higher-level knowledge that she had proven abilities to master. It has meant our child has had the means to develop her God-given potential. Radical acceleration has allowed us to parent a happy child soaring to the heights of her abilities and at the speed she was capable of maintaining. Good grades and cumulative grade-point averages have meant less to me than having a happy child who is confident, self-assured, and just "feels normal." The next phase of Sara's education includes limited access at the upper-division level (Sara's age), lack of scholarships (Sara's age), and inability to access campus student housing (Sara's age). The ability to fund Sara's next level of higher learning will be a challenge but, "God is able to make all grace (every favor and earthly blessing) come to you in abundance, so that you may always and under all circumstances and whatever the need be self-sufficient." Further, God "will also provide and multiply your resources ... and increase the fruits of your righteousness." (2 Corinthians 9:8, 10 AMP). In spite of what sometimes appears a bleak outlook, I believe (have faith) that Sara will continue to receive educational opportunities that are right for her because my faith (trust in God) tells me so. There have been times when I felt my faith has been the only constant support on this journey. Other times I wondered where my faith had gone! By faith, I do believe that whatever God's plan is for Sara's future education it will be accomplished. By faith, I trust He will provide necessary funding to whichever school He wants Sara to attend next (like most parents, I do have a soft spot for one). As Sara prepares for her future, it is comforting to know God has always been in control. "I have directed you in the way of wisdom; I have led you in upright paths. When you walk, your steps will not be impeded; And if you run, you will not stumble. Take hold of instruction; do not let go. Guard her, for she is your life" (Proverbs 4:11–13 NASB).

The unusual education path Sara has taken has often brought exclamations of "You must be so proud of her!" I am proud of the courage Sara has shown to take that "road less traveled" trusting her own intuition of the direction she should go. I am proud that Sara is developing the aptitudes God gave her. Most of all, I am proud and grateful God trusted me to advocate for Sara as a whole person and not just for her special needs in education. I am proud of the young lady she has become and of her personal achievements outside of classrooms as well as those within them. It will be interesting to see what Sara will eventually choose as a major focus of study, and I am eager to see in what ways Sara will impact our world. Wherever the higher level challenge is and whatever her future holds, "I will give thanks to You [God]" for Sara is truly "fearfully and wonderfully made; Wonderful are Your works, And my soul knows it very well" (Psalm 139:14 NASB).

At times, Sara too has reflected on her compulsory education experiences and considered what might come next on her journey.

> The decision to skip high school was probably the best decision I will ever make in my life. Even way back when

I was in elementary school, I knew I was different. I could not relate to other children my age, and I was more comfortable talking with adults anyways. I did not share interests of others, preferring quiet activity to romping and playing. Of course, then I was too young for anyone to make much of a fuss. The school administrators theorized that I would 'even out' as time passed. Sadly, that was not the case. By fifth grade, I had become entirely alienated from my assigned peers. The move from elementary school to middle school only exemplified that alienation, all the way into a passive kind of bullying. I had not been raised with cable television or excessive internet or partying or what-have-you, and the references I did not understand made for much confusion. In addition, I was not only confused by them, but after seeing the influence they had on fellow students, I began to fear and abhor them. Fearing so many of the things my peers took for granted, I was further alienated. I took my plight to my parents, but once again the school barred my path, saying that going to college would deprive me of the necessary socialization. So another year I spent in middle school, a term and place that I had come to hate. I grew depressed, and my grades plummeted. The mundane work was a treacherous bore; the problems were ones I already knew. Towards the end of the year I contemplated suicide, but my religion stayed my hand. After that year, my parents had had enough, and we wrote and mailed petitions. The following college semester, though stressful and new, was a point of change in my life that I will never regret. Sometimes I felt that the world was watching me and judging me, but looking back on it now I take joy in the change. No more was learning strapped down and limited to what was required to pass the test. No more was I stared at and trodden on for being 'different'. Now I was one of them, and I fit in, and I could learn. I moved because I wanted to learn about the world in which I live, and middle school was nothing but a drag to that goal. (Hise, S., 2014)

On May 16, 2014, at age fourteen, Sara made California history when against the grain of a traditional education path, she was conferred two associate degrees: liberal arts in arts and humanities and liberal arts in social and behavioral sciences. Sara became the youngest college graduate in Cerro Coso Community College history as well as the youngest Kern Community College District (KCCD) graduate in their history. Sara has joined very few young California college graduates in the state's history. Interestingly, Kern Community College District (which offers courses in computer science) has not yet determined how to create an "AB2207 Waiver" in its drop-down menu of payment options, to replace what previously had been Sara's concurrent enrollment waiver (which is used for all K–12 students enrolled in college courses). Sara's "free and appropriate education" has been listed as a "bad debt write-off" which is viewable "internally only" because Sara was no longer a concurrently enrolled K–12 student—and "there is no other menu option."

Two months and two days prior to her college commencement at Cerro Coso, Sara was notified of her acceptance into the Program for the Exceptionally Gifted (PEG) at Mary Baldwin College. Designed for young ladies from around the world, PEG provides a secure and supervised residential dormitory for determined, capable, and young students. Sara has most recently expressed growing interest in pursuing double baccalaureate degrees in sociology and studio arts, and perhaps a masters in languages. We are blessed that our daughter has the God-given academic abilities and moral character to meet the very high standards of Mary Baldwin College. Sara will both attend courses at the four-year college level and finally have the opportunity to develop friendships with her *true* peers. She describes the next step in her education future below.

The program for the Exceptionally Gifted is a program directed at teenage girls who are capable of college-level academic study, such as me. I and my parents have found no other program that is better or more likable, and we have found many programs that are not as desirable. I have limited options, and not as much time as I'd like, so I must choose. The PEG program seems to be structured in a way that can sate my academic appetite, and the wide range of degrees and classes offered at Mary Baldwin College suggests that I will be able to explore well beyond my current interests. My interests span a wide area, from art to creative writing to sociology. I'd like to write a few novels when I get the chance, and though I'm not actively looking to get a career in sociology, the field itself is interesting enough to warrant a look. In art I would like to pursue both freehand drawing and traditional animation, as well as learn about and utilize pottery, sculpture, and perhaps metalworking. If possible, I will pursue careers as an author and artist, and my academic interests reflect this goal. Not only does Mary Baldwin have classes pertaining to these interests, but the structure of the PEG program is designed to aid people of my age and ability level. Therefore, I find it appropriate to take advantage of this tailored academic opportunity. It isn't often that we are able to find situations which are so well off. (Hise, S., 2014)

I am grateful for the tremendous forward thinking of Mary Baldwin College, that established PEG and Early College Academy and provides learning opportunities where other institutions are unable or unwilling. I am greatly comforted knowing the experienced staff and instructors have proven successful in meeting the advanced academic special needs of a remarkable and underserved population of students. I do not know if Mary Julia Baldwin (Baldwin College, 1880) and California's Baldwin (sponsor of AB 2207) are related. I do not know who at MBC had the foresight to establish the specialized program for gifted, young female students nearly three decades ago. A women's four-year college (est. 1842), a specialized program for the young and gifted (est. 1985), and a law providing K–12 exemption (adopted 2000) were established in that order. These three things are the exact provisions *His* child on the opposite side of America would require decades later! I do not believe in coincidences as remarkable as these. In order to develop the attributes she was created with, God's provision has always been in play for the child He gave me!

Sometimes I was drawn nearer my faith when it appeared the education climate would never thaw. Other times, I was drawn toward my faith in an almost boastful valiant victory. Neither was appropriate giving honor and glory to God for His blessings upon us or for the battles He had already won on our behalf. Understanding that Jesus chose disciples from the poor, the unclean, and the despised has comforted me. God never needed me to be a perfect Christian—just a responsive one! I have often wondered of the importance of faith to Sara. Have I done enough to instruct Sara and direct her toward a life of faith in Christ? Recently, Sara was asked to describe an experience that forced her to consider two or more equally compelling ideas or points of view and what she learned from her internal struggle. Her response warmed my heart and caused me to grin quite broadly.

One of the most difficult problems I've had to face is pitting my religion against another, one called evolution. I call evolution a religion because religion is based in belief; if no one believes, any religion will cease to be. The evolutionary theory is believed by many to be fact, and yet much of this theory is based in other theories and speculation, not to mention that no one was there to witness it. Likewise, Christianity is based in belief, and no one alive today was there to witness it. However, through the encouragement of my parents, I used my own mind to figure out which theory I thought most correct. My search has led me to discover that many of the facts supporting the evolutionary theory in textbooks today are actually false, some having been proven wrong up to over one hundred years ago. I have found several hoaxes (which were publicly recognized then) still in textbooks today, with impressionable youngsters none the wiser. But, that was only half of my search. In looking for facts about Christianity, I found several theories which showed facts about our earth today fitting in with events described in the Bible. These theories do not stretch my imagination like those of evolution, and they also do not stretch the earth to great age and strange origin. In addition, the scientific theories about Christianity do not surmise that I am descended from a monkey, which I find quite insulting. Am I biased? Perhaps, but from reconciling evolution with my own religion I have learned two things. The first is to use my own mind, in any situation, and not just take for granted what other people tell me. The other is that forcing other people to swallow my religion will never make them believe it, much as evolution has failed to convert me. (Hise, S., 2014)

I am comforted to know that Sara does in fact have an understanding of the Christian faith and the ability to compare it to other beliefs. She knows what she believes and why she believes it. She has developed more self-confidence, she is more accepting of her intellectual abilities, and she has learned to advocate for her own needs and desires. I have no doubt Sara will also be able to argue for her faith positions (apologetics) when she is called to do so or when the discussion arises. Just as my other children are, Sara is a unique and God-inspired individual!

As she continues to mature, Sara is applying to life the equestrian rules her riding instructor, horse trainer, and mentor, Candee Coffee, has taught her. Sara "gathers up and gets organized." She "looks ahead" at where she wants to go, and she "maintains impulsion." I am certain with her growing confidence that Sara will continue to jump over obstacles placed on the course of her life. She has proven herself able to use skills she has while also developing new ones. She has shown dedication in her advanced learning opportunities, and fearlessness in taking on a variety of challenges. Her interests are wide and varied, and she is eager to seek new knowledge and develop new skills.

Art has always been a passion of mine. Added to my affinity for storytelling and character development, it is a powerful tool. In time, I'd like to pursue a definite career with traditional or 2-D animation. Traditional animation is very different from 3-D animation in that each frame is hand drawn, like a giant computerized flipbook. That means that even an animation which is only a few minutes long will consist of hundreds of individual frames, all of which must be cleaned (the animation notes taken out, the lines straightened and thinned, the movement made easy to follow), colored (consistent to each characters individual coloration, following the movement of the skin), and shaded (essential to making the passage of time, the general movement of the characters, and the mood of the entire scene understood). While that does seem a bit daunting, I think I'll welcome the challenge. In addition, part of animation is developing characters and storyline. Without a story to follow, one has nothing to animate. I have always loved creating stories. I also have a knack for creating characters and putting them in challenging, engaging scenarios. That is the basis of all animated shows and movies. [...] When I have gained enough experience I will be able to delve into the career market and have plenty of opportunities. Then I will be able to enjoy my job and my career, rather than to flip pizzas or sort books all day. Doing what you love is preferable to doing something you hate. (Hise, S., 2014)

Dr. Palmer once remarked, "Eventually we all become adults," and I have no doubt Sara will have many opinions about her journey to adulthood and her life experiences throughout childhood. Perhaps one day Sara will indeed pen fiction books. Perhaps at least one will be loosely based on her educational experiences. Perhaps someday she will create a beautiful animated movie, appropriate for all ages, and with a "road less traveled" moral to the story. I think a character (book or movie) based upon me could be a lovely and a fearsome dragon!

In spite of all we have experienced (and Sara has accomplished on this journey), there remains, even today, naysayers and those with negative opinions about Sara's education route (even among the faithful). It is hurtful to hear children question, "Why do you want to send Sara away? Don't you want her anymore?" That anyone, child or adult, would think we would not want to share each possible moment of our daughter's childhood generates profound sadness in me. The reality is that doing what is best for Sara means that her father and I will sacrifice our opportunity to parent our daughter four years sooner than we imagined. I am astounded by the many adults who still do not understand our unconventional decisions and burst forth with unflattering comments. Then I am reminded of Hannah. Hannah took her only son, the toddler Samuel, as soon as he was weaned and left him *forever* in the temple with Eli, the priest (1 Samuel 1:22 NASB). This must have appeared strange and unconventional to other mothers in Hannah's culture and time. Yet Samuel had a purpose to accomplish for God, just as we all do. At the temple and under the instruction of his teacher, Eli, Samuel was able to receive the best preparation possible for accomplishing God's purpose. At Mary Baldwin College, while under the instruction of professors experienced in teaching exceptional (and young) pupils and with the supervision of staff trained to house and counsel the bright young ladies in their care, Sara will receive the best preparation for accomplishing God's plan for her life. My leaving her in the care of collegiate strangers has nonetheless been unconventional and scrutinized. I look forward to where and how we may see all the ways God uses Sara to accomplish His perfect plan. Journaling Sara's educational experience has led me to rediscover some of Sara's own written accounts and perceptions of her childhood. I think they are much more interesting and eloquent than my words about her. The following letter was submitted and chosen by the Kern County California 4-H Extension Office to be forwarded to United States senators, members of congress, and the California Assembly in July 2013. The intent was to inform our elected officials about the benefits of 4-H Cooperative Youth Extension Programs. It also provides greater insight into my daughter's heart than my own words could ever convey.

MY STORY

2012 / 2013 Program Year

Sara Hise

My name is Sara Hise. I have been in my local 4-H club since its beginning in 2009. I am now thirteen years old. When I joined Ridgerunners 4-H Club at its beginning, there were a lot of kinks to work out. In the four years since then, there have been many improvements. 4-H has become a very enjoyable experience for me. While 4-H may not directly influence them, I have several hobbies. First, I collect bottle caps. I have over five hundred of them. A lot of people ask me, "What are you going to do with them?" The answer is, "I'm not doing anything with them. Do you have to do something with the things you collect?" Another hobby is art. As long as I can remember I've always loved to draw. Much of the things I draw are fantasy-based creatures like dragons, but I also draw pictures of the characters I've made up myself. I also experiment with animation quite a bit. A third hobby is writing. By far this is my favorite pastime. I plan to be an author someday. I must have five or six plots to write, and all of them are either fantasy or science-fiction. As you can see, I'm very much into fiction!

The 4-H projects I took this year were Horse, Dog, Leadership, and Crafts and Service. All of them taught me something, and I managed to reach every goal in every project. It took some work, but I was able to do it! In the Horse Project, I ride (and own) my Arabian gelding. His name is Catch Ya Later, and he was named that for a good reason. He holds a track record at both Sacramento and Fresno race tracks. His records have not been broken even after being retired and rehomed to me for the past eight years. Looking at my bay horse nowadays, you'd never guess his speedy history. He has a black mane and tail and three white socks, and a white blaze down his forehead and over his muzzle. He works in both English and Western disciplines and has won several first place awards under both saddles. I think my favorite thing to do, and his favorite as well, is jumping. Catch is worth every penny my parents have invested in him and every minute I have spent with him. In Dog Project, I have my very own shelter rescue dog. He is registered in AKC as a purebred Miniature Pinscher. He is the single most adorable thing on planet Earth. He is three years old. He stands about a foot high at the shoulder and is known as a red stag, where the fur is reddish-brown with a black-tinted stripe down the middle and light red highlights on his shoulders. He also has green eyes, three-inch-high ears and a six-inch-long curly tail which he isn't supposed to have. Most Min Pins get their tails docked and their ears cropped, but since Wesley was a shelter puppy, he didn't have any of that happen to him.

If I were given the choice to relive this year, I wouldn't. The learning experiences I have had in 4-H are moments that deserve to stand for all time, and need no changes. The skills I have learned, such as sociability, will aid me as I ride the great roller coaster called life. My projects did not grow much in size from the previous year, but since I had advanced levels in Horse and Dog, those projects grew in scope for me. I delved far deeper into each respective world than my previous years in 4-H. Since I am only thirteen years old, my parents arranged the purchases of various leashes, collars, dishes, treats, halters, saddles, and so on, but my college textbooks and fees combined with my sister's expenses as a full time student at Humboldt State University, meant my parents had to scale back on some things this year. As a result, I was unable to attend as many 4-H dog and horse shows this year as in the past, as well as a few other events.

Since you may be wondering about my "college textbooks and fees," I will tell you a little bit about my education. I should have just completed the 8th grade. Most third or fourth graders begin making friendships and otherwise socializing but I've had trouble fitting in with others of my chronological age ever since I can remember, the worst of it beginning around that time. At first, I just knew that I was different, but the older I got the more the lesson was pounded into me: You are strange. You do not belong here. I had an elementary principal who supported my accelerated needs and I began taking college classes early at the age of nine. I am the youngest student to ever be admitted to Cerro Coso Community College. By the time I reached middle school, I had become so alienated from the other students that I begged my mom to let me escape. It's not easy being different and it's even harder when adults don't believe you know what's best for yourself. It was hard when there was no change in my education situation for two years of middle school. Luckily my mother and my Horse Project Leader had formed Ridgerunners 4-H and I began to socialize with others who were also interested in new learning challenges.

My Horse Project leader, Candee Coffee, was both willing to teach me when I was there and understand when I couldn't make meetings due to my classes. My Dog Project leader, Coleen Minnick, helped me fill out entries for dog shows I could attend and taught me so much about understanding Wesley's behavior. She calls him the "squeak toy" because he's so small and he focuses best when I have a squeaky toy to keep his attention. These adult leaders have both been great influences on me, always encouraging me to do my best and never give up. All of my club members have been there for me; when I couldn't remember my Dog Project reports and listening even when I forgot to bring all the materials for my demonstrations. 4-H has given me acceptance for who I am and encouragement to become whatever I choose to be.

One of the things I have had a lot of trouble with for most of my life is leadership. To me, leadership means listening to and taking the opinions of those in your group, while still being strong enough to make difficult decisions against judgments of those who disagree with you. When I am in charge, I constantly second guess myself and end up looking back at my choices as bad ones. 4-H has really helped me overcome my self-consciousness. When I made my decisions, my friends in 4-H were quick to support me and stand beside me. Though I believe I will never quite be comfortable in a leader's position, I am much more capable than I was last year. As for citizenship, I've learned that self-sacrifice is often the most valued trait among a group, and so it's a good thing to have as a citizen. But citizenship isn't just about sacrificing things for others. It's also about helping others and upholding the goals of your group. This year we made cookies for several organizations in our town, including the Fire Department, Police Department, and Animal Shelter. After that, we decorated clay pots and planted flowers in them to give as gifts to the local senior citizens assisted living facility. This supported the goals of our group by proving that we are not only here as a youth development organization, but also to improve and aid our community.

Still worried about my troubles in school, my parents sought the advice of an expert who specialized in education for youth like me. They filed petitions which allowed me to be admitted to college in a full-time status. Now, well, I've got it made here in college. Lots of learning challenges, fun and friends, but there is one little catch. In all the wide U. S. A. there is exactly one university that appears to be the perfect fit for me—and may accept me after I graduate from Cerro Coso in May of 2014. This wonderful university is in Virginia. I will be leaving my little town of Ridgecrest, California next year, so this has been my very last year to fully take part in the 4-H club I've come to love and cherish. Without my 4-H club, I'm not certain I would have ever made it this far in my college work. I am planning to register for the 4-H 2013 / 2014 program year but I know my participation will be limited and I will not be able to accomplish nearly as much as I have in the past four years. I believe this is my last record book submission and I want to say that this year was a great year to end my 4-H experience. 4-H has been a wonderful opportunity for me to learn about things that interested me. I know that the leadership skills I will always remember are the caring and connection I received from my leaders and my friends. Now is the time for me to seek new learning opportunities, and I know my club and leaders will be cheering for me wherever my opportunities take me—to Virginia and beyond. I will miss Wesley and Catch most of all, but I know I will enjoy reading my 4-H record book and remembering all the wonderful things I did with them, the skills I have learned and the good friends I have made. (Hise, S., 2013)

As parents, we often question whether our children have absorbed the instructions we have given them. Have we been successful in developing core values? Do they understand the benefits of good manners? Have they learned to appropriately communicate with others in various situations? Did we provide them enough unconditional love, and do they know we accept them just as God made them? Have we taught them to embrace humanity kindly and give compassion? I do not think I am the only mother to ever question the preparedness of my children to embark into the world on their solo adventures, wondering if they would remember to say please and thank you, and keep their sarcasm in check! I have yet to meet any parent who never asked their child, "Did you hear me?" This is usually followed by "Are you listening?" Finally comes, "Do you understand what I am saying!" And then comes the day when your child arrives for spring break and presents you with crumpled copy of an oral presentation given in speech class. Our validating confirmation of our efforts to "start up our child in the way she should go" (or at least a validation of our investment in equine feed and care) has arrived! (Proverbs 22:6) Sara's notes from her informative speech presented during her communications course at Mary Baldwin College follows.

TITLE: <u>Horses and Lessons</u>

THESIS STATEMENT: "All humans have the ability to understand the language of horses."

INTRODUCTION:

I. Some of you may have taken riding lessons, or maybe just gone and seen a horse somewhere. It may have been an amazing experience, or it may have been horrid, But did you ever think about it from the horse's point of view? (Catching attention with a rhetorical question).

   A. I remember one time in particular when I had just finished a riding lesson. It was evening when I brought him to his pen and he had dinner in his bucket. I was trying to get his halter off of him when he stomped on my foot, intentionally. I could see the look in his eye; he meant to do it.

   B. However, I did not correct this behavior or scold him, because while I was fussing at his halter he was being made to stand three feet away from his dinner and not eat it. I know I'd stomp some feet to get to my chocolate, so I left him alone on that one (Story hook).

   C. Thesis: If you just take a little time to think about how horses are motivated and how they think, your ability to speak to them will be greatly enhanced, and you will have a greater understanding between you and them.

II. Today I am going to teach you how to begin to understand the language of horses.

    A. I've been riding horses since I was four years old, and I've had (in my humble opinion) a great trainer to do it. I've ridden multiple horses and worked with many more, including working with younger or newer riders and helping them understand how to go about it. I've ridden in shows and gotten all kinds of ribbons and trophies. I've ridden in both English and Western disciplines, and bareback a few times, though I prefer having a saddle. (Establishing credibility).

    B. Over this long period of time, I've picked up certain behaviors that either I can do or the horse will do. These behaviors supply a map for how one should conduct oneself around horses. Communicating with horses involves keeping calm, giving proper cues, and giving praise and punishment at appropriate times. (Preview).

BODY:

I. Keeping calm is the first and most important step to interacting with horses.

    A. A horse will pick up on the general states of those around them, so you can set your horse up for success by being calm and giving the horse support.

    B. Horses will react to stressful situations, and when a horse is stressed their training is replaced by their instincts of being a horse. While the fight or flight reaction is good for keeping a horse alive in a dangerous situation, it is not good for modern purposes.

C. You should keep your hands, feet, and voice quiet. Running and waving your arms around is a sudden movement that can startle a horse. Yelling and hollering is generally not acceptable behavior around horses.(Transition: Keeping calm goes hand in hand with letting the horse know what's going on)

II. If you want to keep your horse calm, you should let your horse know what's happening.

    A. Sound. When approaching a horse, it's a general courtesy to say something, cluck, or whistle.

        1. Something suddenly appearing near them will be taken on instinct as a threat, and the horse may kick or spook.

        2. Clucking is a common form of encouragement among horse people to their horses. It is used in tacking up, riding, and leading.

    B. Sight. Once you have warned the horse that you are coming, you should place yourself in their line of sight, and stay there.

        1. Do not approach from the back or the front. A horse's eyes are set wide apart on its head, so that it can see almost all the way around it, but there

are blind spots directly behind it and under its neck.

2. If a horse cannot see you clearly, it cannot affirm that you are you. You may be a predator, in being sneaky and hiding, and that means that the horse must defend itself.

C. Touch. Even after you have approached the horse, being courteous by remaining close will do a service to you and it.

1. If you must go around behind the horse, keep your hand on its rump to let it know that you are still there. Going under the neck is not recommended!
2. When you pat a horse, be sure that you save rough patting for the main part of the body and the side of the neck. Be gentle with the face and legs.
3. Touch is a very useful communicator for pretty much every action that a horse is required to do on daily basis. If the horse is refusing the bit, tickling the inside of the mouth will encourage them to open wide. The horse will be more obliging in picking the hooves if you run your hand down their leg rather than just grab at their hoof.
(Transition: Once you have set the horse up for success, you can begin to command it.)

III. A horse can only know what actions to perform if trained properly.

    A. Praise should be delivered in an amount that is scaled to what the horse has accomplished.

        1. If the particular horse finds a certain task difficult, it merits a higher level of praise and rewarding. Generalization among individuals should always be kept to a minimum, and this is no different for horses.

        2. If it is a particularly simple task like walking on when kicked or turning when told to by the reins, praise is not needed, and can be saved for when the pattern or section of the lesson has been completed.

    B. Punishment should be delivered only when absolutely necessary, and should be designed for the offense.

        1. If the horse continually refuses to perform a certain task, it is verified as being intentional and can be reprimanded. Once is not enough to verify intent. A jerk on the reins will cause the head to jerk back, which is why it is effective when the horse is eating or biting. However, a refusal to do a certain thing cannot be corrected by the reins. The horse must be made to do the thing that is being refused. A horse will not understand yelling except as something that is dangerous and predatory.

CONCLUSION

I. A horse that is set up for success will succeed, much like a person. The elements for success are easy too, because we already follow them every day. I haven't taught you anything new.

    A. Keeping calm is a necessity for any relationship, with a horse or otherwise. Do you run hooting and hollering into your professor's office to discuss your paper? Or do you walk in, in a calm and controlled fashion?

    B. Letting people know what's going on is what we do all the time, especially in college. What else are lectures? How could you ever join a conversation if you didn't do this?

    C. Praise and punishment are universally known for needing to be executed properly. If professors gave bad grades on good papers, would college have any merit? Talking to horses uses many of the very same mannerisms that we employ as polite human beings. If we're polite to horses too, every riding lesson will be far better for all involved. Since everyone already does it, everyone has the ability to do it

II. In return for being set up to succeed, and thus giving us the best lesson possible, horses teach us all valuable life lessons.

    A. Predators could be hiding around every corner, just waiting to take a bite out of you, so always look before you leap.

B. At the end of the day, after the bitter breakups and sorrowful tales, and the horrid injuries, and the mournful losses, there are still pens full of manure to clean, so suck it up and get 'er done. Whining ain't never got no manure moved.

C. When I committed to a ride, and said I'd be there, I rode and my horse was there with me. It has taught me dedication—no matter the weather, no matter what had happened in our lives, no matter how well we did or how prepared we were, no matter the soreness of my toe, we rode.

D. The most important lesson was the one my horse taught me every day, rain or shine, wind or without, bad day or not. It was the lesson he taught me with an affectionate nicker whether or not I was wearing those stuffy, sparkly, stiff show-clothes or just jeans and an old T-shirt. It was the lesson that we are told about every day by other people but never seem to learn. My horse taught me by his actions, because whatever I looked like on the outside, he still trusted and loved the person underneath.

Photo Credit: Jenny Hazlewood

Gifted and Talented Education: Truth or Fiction?

We wanted Sara to receive challenging learning experiences and to have social engagement with peers her age. However, she craved a faster-paced and advanced level of instruction and like-minded peers regardless of their age differences. In fact, Sara emotionally, physically, and mentally required the intriguing and stimulating mental challenges! Didn't her middle school have a GATE program? The principal replied, "We *do* have a GATE program. There are a lot of smart kids in band." This is a good example of how individual administrators can interpret what *enrichment* is and determine what level is sufficient for *all* gifted students. This school enrolled "smart kids in band." Sara was in the band, but does that mean band was appropriate *enrichment* for gifted students? Perhaps the administrator's statement meant band is only for "smart kids." Or perhaps all smart kids are in the top two-percent of IQ scores? Maybe she meant that gifted students always play musical instruments? Parents are frequently frustrated by employees in education who too often disregard their inquiries or sidestep questions.

Many will argue that our government has now (and has had for many decades) an active Gifted and Talented

Education Program (GATE) and that existing program should be sufficient for all students who place anywhere in the ranges: gifted, highly gifted, profoundly or exceptionally gifted, or talented. Not only is this a huge variety of abilities, levels of interests, and IQ testing scores, but the very existence of GATE is largely a myth.

> At present, nearly half of all gifted students are underachievers. There is no federal legislation that mandates gifted education nor are there cohesive infrastructures in place that help parents recognize – and take advantage of – resources to effectively advocate for gifted children. The absence of such practices stifles the development of highly intelligent youth, a population the Davidson Institute asserts is one of the most underserved populations in American schools today, and poses significant concerns regarding the development of future advances and inventions in all fields of study. (Institute n.d.)

The choking of our bright future has become our "normal" education policy and one that unifies our nation. I am appalled by the consistent failure to embrace the attributes and abilities of students with the capability to better our nation and our world. Yet, our legislators and education budgets have continued to do so.

> there is no federal mandate for gifted education. But if we recognize the importance of special programs for students whose atypical brains encode less-accepted

differences, we should extrapolate to create programs
for those whose atypical brains encode remarkable
abilities. (Solomon, *Far from the Tree*, 457)

Nationally, the brightest and most capable of our young
students receive zero dollars to assist them with more
challenging curriculum or faster-paced curriculum. This
population of our nation's youth are victims to this void in our
federally funded public education system, and the vacuum
that has sucked up their constitutionally guaranteed "free
and *appropriate* education." Those children (without furious
advocates) too often sacrifice their potentials and succumb
to depressed and disengaged education experiences. Many
people presume state government funds services for gifted
students in their state's public schools. It is unlikely that the
economic priorities in any state's education system include
the relatively small percentage of students who are gifted
when compared to the majority of pupils' unmet needs in
their underfunded public schools. The greater likelihood
is that all states that once had gifted programs but have
slashed education budgets now have gifted services as extinct
as dinosaurs.

In 1961, the California Legislature established
the Mentally Gifted Minor (MGM) program for
students scoring in the 98th percentile or above on
standardized intellectual ability tests [...] Assembly
Bill (AB) 1040, enacted in 1980 established the
GATE program allowing districts to set their own
criteria for entrance. AB 1040 expanded service

beyond the intellectually gifted to students who were gifted and talented in areas such as specific academic ability, leadership, visual and performing arts, and creativity. In 2000, two pieces of legislation were enacted that amended provisions of the *EC* [Education Code] for GATE. AB 2313 amended *EC* 52200 requiring that GATE programs be planned and organized as differentiated learning experiences within the regular school day and established a GATE funding formula based on the average daily attendance for all students in the district. AB 2207 amended *EC* 48800 providing options for gifted and talented pupils to attend classes at postsecondary institutions regardless of the pupil's age or grade level. (C. D. Education n.d.)

Most of us are not lawyers, but as near as I can decipher California recognized (in 1961) the small portion of students in the top two percent (2%) of intellectual ability. The state established a program aptly named the Mentally Gifted Minor Program (MGM). MGM specifically targeted these highly intellectual students. Ten years later, Paul D. Plowman provided a report on the Mentally Gifted Minor Program to the California Department of Education.

The State of California encourages school districts to provide qualitatively different and uniquely appropriate learning experiences for children in the upper two percent of general mental ability. Through guide-lines, consultant service, and extra funds, the state seeks (1) to prepare over 100,000 mentally gifted minors for responsible and productive adult roles in government, business, and the professions; (2) to help each gifted child gain a realistic and healthy concept of himself--his strengths, his weaknesses, his areas of needed improvement, and his potentialities; and (3) to develop these children into intellectually and creatively capable, productive, and compassionate human beings. (Plowman, 1)

In 1971, it had been established that across the state of California, more than one hundred thousand gifted students had "special needs," that they should be "targeted" for "appropriate learning experiences," and that their abilities should be "encouraged" to be nurtured. Mr. Plowman's report explained,

> Furthermore, it can be said that programs for gifted children are consistent with basic principles of American education and of American democracy and that such programs are logically a part of a broader concern for optimum development or full development of all children with special talents and special needs. (Plowman 1971)

This report to the California Department of Education (which can be accessed and viewed entirely online through ERIC—the Education Resources Information Center) makes clear that, in fact, giftedness is as much an educational special need as any other. It also cautioned the California

Department of Education about diverting funding away from
the special needs of the gifted.

> With the increasing number of financial problems
> experienced by school districts, attention may be
> diverted away from special program development and
> directed more toward the regular program which may
> be just as inappropriate for the gifted as it is for the
> borderline mentally retarded child. (Plowman, 16)

Nineteen years after legislation that had established MGM,
the state of California legislators threw out a new name,
GATE, and permitted its individual school districts the
power to decide who would be admitted into local programs
(AB 1040). At this same time, California also expanded its
target pupils from the two percent academically minded to
incorporate "talented" pupils (to be determined by individual
school districts' staffs). In keeping with its apparent twenty-
year revision plan, in 2000, California passed AB 2313.
This mandated that GATE learning experiences be planned,
organized, differentiated, and occur during the regular school
day, while also setting a state-funding formula for GATE
based on daily attendance of *all* students within individual
school districts. This was also the same year AB 2207 passed
the California Assembly (sponsored by Baldwin). Does this
mean gifted and talented students are benefiting from
programs that meet their needs? No! If we continue reading
the fine print of California legislation, we can understand
why the needs of this population are frequently not met at

all or met with great discrimination between schools and school districts.

> governing boards that elect to provide programs may establish program for gifted and talented students consisting of special day classes, part-time groupings and cluster groupings (C. D. Education n.d.)

It has been fifty-two years since the state of California acknowledged high achieving and highly intellectual youth had special needs (1961). California's legislators have repeatedly passed *new* laws regarding GATE, and each has been adopted into California Department of Education code. These later pieces of legislation have created something of a patchwork and do not help the gifted since the law continues to ignore the special needs of these children. Current education code *now* allows school districts that "elect to provide" gifted special needs *may* do so, and those who decline to establish programs are not mandated to. When it comes to special needs, the powers that be have established mandatory assistance programs for some and an *optional* program to assist the gifted. Mr. Plowman reported in 1971 "that programs for gifted children are consistent with basic principles of American education and of American democracy." California's basic principles of education and our federal educational funding have clearly ignored Mr. Plowman's findings reported to the California Department of Education. When compared to other leading nations of the world, the United States has been consistently dropping in educational performances for decades. Perhaps the elephant in the room that no one wants to see is the "basic principles of American education" have been lost in repetitive legislation (Plowman). Gifted students are not the only ones being shortchanged. California is currently ranked forty-eighth in our nation for public K–12 education. Still, some education experts and legislators continue to cling to perceived superiority in thinking they know the best decisions to make regarding our students. Clearly it's not working! Plowman had cautioned that "financial difficulties could divert funding away from gifted programs inappropriately." Indeed! They certainly have just as Mr. Plowman predicted.

California's *optional* GATE program has resulted in widespread discrimination. There is no fairness or equality in the distribution of learning opportunities at advanced levels when each school's administrator possesses the power to deny meeting gifted pupils' special needs. The major determining factor is of course dollars. Dollars change from year to year based upon each district's pupil enrollment. Each school will receive more or less dollars based on their student population. Sara's elementary school population was largely underprivileged, with few families able to donate to fundraisers or join Parent-Teacher Associations (PTAs). The neighboring elementary school (approximately two miles away) had a hugely successful Parent-Teacher Organization (PTO) with a treasury of thousands of dollars. Their PTO could more regularly afford to support challenging enrichment for gifted pupils at its campus. In California, GATE is a dead acronym. It is a Department of Education *optional* program supported by *surplus* dollars (that do not exist) and administered by *subjective* authority figures who are often ignorant of the diagnosed needs of truly gifted students. As long as there is no federal mandate for funding gifted education our nation's potential will continue to be academically undernurtured. As long as California's and our nation's GATE programs remain unfunded or underfunded *and* at the discretion of each individual school district, GATE will never be a standardized or sustained instruction (the free and **appropriate** education) meeting the special needs of our gifted pupils. Our legislature has recognized the need, our federal constitution has guaranteed to provide appropriate education, and a mythical program has been adopted into law—a law that provides for highly intellectual youth or youth with exceptional talent in specific areas *only* if school boards "elect to provide" programs in their individual districts. Our local school district goes the extra mile and also provides administrators the freedom to define what constitutes "enrichment." GATE is discriminatory. Gifted and talented students *do* have special needs that will not be met by a grouping together in the band class. Our personal experience and my research shows many public educational programs are often nothing more than ineffective words on paper. Parents must be keenly aware in order to advocate for unmet needs and legal benefits. GATE may exist in your own school or district (you should investigate programs in your area for yourself), but in our rural and unfunded school district, GATE is a ghost program. A program that has been financially cut and redefined, it is as effective as the disappearing ink with which it was written. Plowman's 1971 report provided to the state of California's Department of Education said, "programs for gifted children are consistent with basic principles of American education and of American democracy." This is an example of why we pray for our country!

California's convoluted GATE program also delays in identifying students and providing higher-level challenges to them at earlier ages. The current ineffective GATE program does not evaluate and target students for (administrator-defined) enrichment opportunities until they have begun the fourth grade. The explanation given by educators and administrators is, "Some students begin school as accelerated learners and level off." This is contradictory to all the research I have done. It has been my experience that the vast majority of those working in education will make certain that you know *they* are the education professionals and *you* are the parent. As a parent, I believe it is ludicrous to persist in a delay of four or five years with students who were accelerated when they began their formal education. Many agree with me, since research has shown that a child held back academically from what they might have achieved promotes loss of interest. Too often bright and curious minds succumb to huge blocks of time in which gifted students experience boredom while waiting for the class to catch up to where they are (as was the case with our daughter). Some may even have begun disrupting class out of frustration. Take a look at this excerpt from the book *Guiding the Gifted Child.*

> In many instances it is a matter of *how* boys and girls are going to be taught rather than *what* they are going to be taught. So far, little attention has been paid to this phase of education with the result that

many gifted children end up in the ranks of the early school dropouts. For example, a large number of boys and girls enter Kindergarten and first grade with an overwhelming desire to learn. Some of the gifted pupils will actually be reading and will, therefore, require little in the way of readiness work to prepare them for formal learning skills that they may still have to perfect. However, some of their motivation will soon be lost unless they are given ample opportunity to achieve success commensurate with their accomplishment quotients. To hold all students to the same pattern of class instruction and the same work materials is a great waste (Thomas, 24).

In 1966 experts were advising educators and parents not to hold back advanced learners as early as kindergarten and first grade lest they lose motivation! Today, educators justify this very thing and call it "leveling out." Our current system stifles bright youngsters and sends them down the standard conveyer belt through each grade level because that is what we have always done. What does more than fifty years of research show? It shows some gifted students will refuse to perform at their actual ability levels (as ours did) and intentionally "dumb down," which in professional terms is called *disengaging* (Palmer, 115). Our federal and state departments of education need to understand that the eight words indicating any organization is in decline are "but we have always done it this way." It is not *only* in the classroom where changes need to be addressed, but also in the bureaucracy where the trickle-down effect began.

GATE listed on paperwork is no guarantee there is an actual program in force that is meeting student needs. Current, prior, and ongoing economic cuts to education have resulted in a huge disparity between school districts statewide and even between individual schools within the same district. Those schools that have high-income-earning parents and active Parent-Teacher Associations (PTAs) or Parent-Teacher-Student Organizations (PTSOs) support are more likely to have active GATE programs while their counterparts (those in blighted or rural areas) are less likely to have alternative fundraising to support GATE learning opportunities. Gifted students account for such a small fraction of the overall student body that they are not the priority when it comes to budgeting. California Department of Education's "self-governing" endows each school district with the authority to determine how it will best serve its own district's student body with the funding it receives thus resulting in huge disparity of programs and services offered between districts. Districts determine if they will *offer* GATE, who will administrate it if they do, and how it might be budgeted. In our district, each school principal has the responsibility to provide the best programs he/she can within his/her individual school's budget, perhaps relying on a pittance of discretionary funds to provide any gifted and talented pupils with some discretionary enrichment. This all leads to the bottom line: the minority few with the greatest ability to grasp higher-level academics, to process challenging concepts with ease of comprehension, and to retain learned information may receive the least opportunity to achieve their full educational potential—due to geography!

As long as this discrimination exists wherein the wealthy schools or districts have and the poor schools and districts have not, society will lose the benefits of great minds that succumbed to standardized boredom and settled for less than what they might have achieved.

Photo Credit: Laurrie Pollock

TEN

A Mother's Observations

As I have stated previously, I never imagined I would spend countless hours, days, and certainly not years researching the history of assembly bills and education codes. After a long look at California's past and present educational decisions and national education decisions, I am amazed how many problems exist within our public education system. Public education had been an area I had trusted our elected legislators and educators to manage. I am now aware of the existence of numerous areas of failure. Education oversights, overreaching policies, micromanagement, and underfunding are strangleholds on our nation's students. Our departments of education are aware of low performance statistics and their devastating results to our communities and to society as a whole. Budget cuts to education have continued at all-time highs, and funding for gifted students is not likely to miraculously appear from either state or federal levels.

Common Core State Standards

On the premise of standardizing student-learning objectives nationally, our legislators made the decision to spend taxpayer dollars on new Common Core State Standards

(CCSS) curriculum. So far, the introduction of CCSS appears to be a national nightmare. Proponents of the CCSS claim it is teaching students better critical-thinking skills. Opponents claim it is indoctrinating an entire generation of our nation and removing free-thinking. A major area that *has* remained consistent is American students testing lower than foreign students in core subjects. This is one reason why the CCSS curriculum was initiated. There are many areas of the new standards material that are concerning, changes in terminology and in textbook materials. Language arts instructions in primary grades has disturbed many parents. Mathematics terminology as well has changed. *Minus* and *take away* are terms no longer appropriate for use in second-grade subtraction. Instructors now teach the term *take apart*. Some students (and parents) are confused by this change (referencing it to fractions). Some grandmothers think they could teach this level of math for pennies on the dollar. "Honey, Grandma made you four cookies, eat one then count again—that's subtraction!" CCSS is using new terms and methods for math addition as well. Grandma is not saying, "I'm so proud," when second graders tell her she is adding two and two incorrectly because she is supposed to separate 2 into "doubles" (1+1) then add the doubles, 1+1 and 1+1. CCSS is no doubt confusing some students, aggravating some instructors, and angering many parents. Proponents believe that CCSS will improve overall education nationally because it will standardize minimum requirements across the country. Opponents believe many students are receiving less subject attention from instructors who have been increasingly mandated by legislation resulting in them *teaching to the test*.

What is most suitable for all students is to thoroughly learn subjects, not to be overwhelmed with knowing all possible methods of obtaining the correct answer because all methods will be on a standardized test! Many parents are alarmed by this standardized curriculum where expectations remain age/grade-based and are strictly enforced. The student in inner city Detroit, Michigan, likely has educational needs vastly different from the student in affluent Santa Monica, California. CCSS mandates interventions for struggling students, but where will those intervention helps come from, how beneficial will they be, and is it right to hold all students to the same mandated time frame for attaining the same level of standardized achievement? Many parents and schools across the nation have been choosing opt out of CCSS. The basics in education were once taught with instructors giving knowledge in subjects that all students would thoroughly understand and master (or repeat course work until they had). As time has passed, basic subject materials *have* changed. There is more information to convey to students, more material to teach, and new testing to measure achievements. American parents I have spoken with want to get children reading ***and*** comprehending the vocabulary words on the page and focus on thoroughly covering subject materials like science, history, and math. The objectives of the Common Core State Standards appear written to express this as well. Parents I know are concerned with preparing their students for success in life—with the ability to balance checkbooks and live within their means by maintaining appropriate debt-to-income ratios (something our elected officials have not been able to do nationally and in many states). Parents are also concerned about the opportunities their children will have in the work force of the future as many are struggling with their own employment options presently. CCSS focus is on age/grade time frames, which is typical of how our education system operates. CCSS is our latest *new* way to spend tax dollars on an education fix that so far is not. All of our students (not just disengaged gifted ones) are in jeopardy of being underachievers in a system where decisions are being made by a huge and impersonal government. CCSS is only one controversial area of public education concern. Many appear to be concerned about the "standards," but we should not forget about the *time*. Students need the amount of time each requires to understand and achieve success at his or her personal rate of speed—whether slower or faster than their age/grade peers. Successful learning is the mastery of the material studied—in as much time as individual students require to achieve it. As long as we are an age/grade-based education system, we will have students who need more or less time to achieve success, which makes the strictly enforced CCSS all the more unpopular.

Instruction

In my opinion, our current educational mandates combined with minimal subject exposure correlate to the graduation of young voters who have received inadequate instruction in subjects of American government and civics, political science, and United States history. Other areas also suffer from rapid exposure. This is bad for our future as a nation! It is unconscionable that as a nation we are issuing high school diplomas to young Americans who have been rapidly exposed to subjects that previous generations were thoroughly taught and had fully understood! Today's public education system does not allow deep study in areas where students may have interest or a passion for further understanding, or where they would benefit from more subject instruction in an area of difficulty. Instructors must move on to the next area on the test! It is doubtful that I am alone in my thinking that our young people deserve the best preparation for their paths in life to become contributors to society and to impact our world for the better. How can our youth compete globally when our preparation system has micromanaged their teachers with mandate upon mandate (actually diminishing quality teacher to student interactions)? Today's young people will be casting votes for future elected officials who will amend, initiate new, and repeal current laws that will govern all. Sooner rather than later, we will be at the mercy of their worldviews, their moralities, and their impacts upon the governmental balance of power and freedoms America has always known. I would prefer American students obtain thorough subject instruction that prepares them for their future life privileges and their responsibilities. I do not believe I am alone in thinking this. There are responsibilities that require the use of good reasoning skills, application of excellent research practices, ability to comprehend detailed written documents with advanced vocabulary, and expressing oneself as a well versed and competent person. All of these skills, together with a thorough knowledge in American government, prepare those with voting rights to elect (or become) great future leaders. I think our public education instruction of our future national decision makers should include more than California's high school minimum requirement of "a one-semester course in American government and civics."[11] The total instructional hours California high school students spend learning about their national government are less than the instructional time required for students to attain a provisional driver's permit. (State Minimum Course Requirements n.d.)

I believe that many educators are unhappy being restricted to teaching in a manner to satisfy the law and to accomplish all the requirements demanded of it. Educators who would love to teach subjects by spending more time on topics where children show enthusiasm to learn (as well as areas where some students have trouble) are too often compelled to move on to other areas too soon. Teachers are constrained by laws that drive them to provide rapid instruction and focus time on ensuring that their students will pass required standardized testing. Our teachers, schools, and districts must *prove* students have achieved minimum knowledge in compulsory subject areas in order to maintain the flow of decreased financial funding, keep in the good graces of their local districts, and adhere to departments of education mandates. This means that teachers have limited time to spend on areas not covered on standardized tests and often no time at all. Many excellent teachers have left the profession because of these constraints and the better benefits, higher salaries, and job security that working elsewhere provides.

---

[11] One semester of American government and civics, one semester of United States history and one semester of economics are required to meet the California Department of Education high school graduation requirement in social studies.

It would be ideal if teachers were able to convey knowledge in subject matters they felt passionate about while also earning a suitable living, receiving deserved respect, and being blessed with a classroom full of well-behaved, eager learners. Yes, that would be ideal. Sadly those elements are now largely, if not entirely, absent from our public schools. Remember the days when teachers had the time to work with their students and students revered their teacher for the special attention? Teachers are spending more time than ever before in an attempt to handle the diversity of needs in their classrooms. Student disruptions play a large role in time wasting and inhibit the learning process from being all that it could be for others. I am wholly in agreement that each child should have his or her educational needs met. Our classroom sizes are large, our pupils sometimes unruly, and our expectations of teacher achievements high. It is a rare human who chooses to enter this profession. I find it sad that teachers must have signed, written contracts with parents, must accommodate disobedient children, and are remanded to instruct for standardized test requirements at government mandated time frames in order that students' learning is "optimal." Our schools cannot provide successful instruction without extremely motivated and genuinely concerned high-achieving teachers, those special instructors who, working in concert with the support of forward thinking administrators, commit to meet each individual student's needs in our nation's public schools. Again, I think these are rare human beings. They are often individuals willing to earn a higher level education and work for a salary that is frequently lower than their own educational achievement peers. There are many choices of careers that pay higher and require the same or less education. When public school teachers leave a profession they once loved to take positions outside the education arena, it begs the question: why wouldn't parents choose an alternative path for their students when even the teachers have abandoned their public education posts? Consider that an individual is offered debt repayment of their educational student loans if they enter and remain in the teaching profession (or other service field) for ten years. This is an undeniable incentive *for* the teaching profession, yet many teachers become exhausted by policy constraints, standardized requirements, and unruly or disobedient students. Many choose to change their careers at the end of ten years teaching—or sooner! I predict that until we give value back to the teaching profession, are willing to keep education off the budget cutting list, and decrease the micromanagement of our qualified instructors, the teaching profession will continue to lose university graduates to jobs in other career fields. Industries with less micromanagement, fewer career threats, more respect, and higher income earnings are far more desirable than teaching to the test under threat of reprimand. Have we forgotten that teachers— who ignite the spark, keep the flame, and motivate a desire for lifelong learners—are great mentors for all our children? The future depends upon an education system that both solicits and retains these remarkable individuals. Teachers should not be enticed to enter this profession to reduce their own educational-loan debt. Neither should they be compelled by burnout to exit the profession they once pursued with passion.

Alternatives and Accommodations

America has become a nation where some parents will do almost anything to obtain an alternative to public education for their child. Some parents use their hard-work ethic or frugal financial planning to ensure their children are able to attend religious or private schools. Some students may obtain benefits from a homeschool situation because they have parents who are able to purchase private curriculum and a parent who has available time to instruct them. Many families don't have or choose those options. Working single parents are some of the most dedicated family men and women I have ever known—few can homeschool their youngsters on their jobsite. California has created a huge disparity in public school education quality between districts and sometimes between schools within the same district. While some may believe that services and options are available to their student, the reality at times is quite disturbing. Some parents residing in some districts may have options to enroll their child in a public school more suited to their abilities or need, such as a magnet school that groups students together by a specific subject focus area. Again, this option is not available to the majority. Only some school districts in some states allow parents to request an interdistrict or intradistrict transfer into another public school they believe would be more appropriate for their students. In our local district, parents may request open-enrollment transfers to schools other than the one their children are zoned for. The approved transfers are determined by seats available each year, and transfer students are chosen by a complicated system similar to winning the lottery. Parents must reapply each year they wish to keep their child in the school they believe is more appropriate. However, there is also a local district policy that prohibits a student from outside a zoned area to "displace" a student zoned for their own neighborhood school. If there is a seat unoccupied in your student's grade-level class at another school, then your child may be approved for a transfer (with no guarantee he or will be permitted to remain there for the entire school year). If a student moves into a neighborhood midyear, your open-enrolled child may be bumped back to the school he or she is zoned for at any time. Adding to parental frustration, our district has published that children bond very quickly to their teachers, so it is important to apply for transfers during summer break so children begin school terms with their teacher. How effective or appropriate is the current open-enrollment option if it places students at risk of relocation after bonding with a teacher and classmates? Some schools within our local district have very active PTO/PTA organizations while other schools in less affluent neighborhoods do not. In example, a musically talented student would benefit from open enrollment to a school where a music program is offered (supported by PTO/PTA funds) in lieu of remaining at his or her zoned campus where the music program has suffered budgetary cuts and has no PTO/PTA to restore it. This is the entire point of open enrollment—to allow student access to schools better suited for them. This type of program in California was initially created to discourage parents from pushing for "vouchers" on voter ballot measures. Vouchers would have given parents ability (equal to what public schools receive per pupil) to place their child an institution of their choice (parochial, private, or specialized) or perhaps use their voucher toward home schooling. Instead, open-enrollment was the policy thrown to the voters to appease them. Open enrollment is not guaranteed, consistent, or secure, but it is *a policy*! Whether we wish to admit it, discrimination in education still exists within our standardized public schools. Our education system authorities may claim otherwise, but the economically disadvantaged *and* intellectually gifted children still receive fewer opportunities to reach their full potential. Students attending public taxpayer-funded schools in more affluent neighborhoods continue to have greater access to programs (through private support). Students attending taxpayer-funded schools in blighted zones have fewer or downgraded opportunities due to budget cuts. Gifted students receive the least. Education issues exist in many forms beyond the recently introduced Common Core State Standards.

Special-Needs Programs

What can parents do when public education is not meeting the needs of their specific student or when parents feel stonewalled by professionals in education? How can we ensure *all* students have access to the best opportunity to advance their individual knowledge at appropriate levels? How do parents know if their child is receiving an appropriate education? For those students with special needs, there are assistance programs available. One is the Individual Education Plan (IEP). The IEP is provided under the federal Individuals with Disabilities Act (IDEA).

It sets goals in a legally binding, written contract that school officials must meet for each student's unique learning needs, thereby assisting student success and potential to pass standardized requirements. Another is the Resource Specialist Program (RSP). This program provides students with learning assistance in specific subjects through the use of one-on-one attention with a school's credentialed teacher in special education. This is designed to provide a student with learning disabilities optimal learning opportunities and preparation to pass standardized requirements. Speech therapists, English as a second language (ESL), and Head Start (preschool) are also programs available to provide assistance toward student success. There are many programs in existence (even after budget cuts) to meet specific needs of students. All are obtained through a process. All involve a combined effort between the school officials, district, and the student's parents. Most also provide a "pull-out" time when the pupil is removed from the teacher's instruction for intervention. When it comes to meeting special needs, our current education regulations have provided a great variety of assistance programs. An adequate program is *not* available to bright minds that excel with minimal assistance, perform above grade level standards with ease, and require a faster pace or more challenging curriculum to maintain their enthusiasm and potential for learning. These are proven special needs that are continuing to be ignored by educators and legislators. Parents of gifted children must advocate for unmet needs of their exceptional children and must be willing to participate in meeting those needs. Parents cannot rely on public education to immediately align or educators to readily join the cause for their individual gifted student. Parents also cannot immediately buckle and accept less than their gifted student's appropriate level of challenge. These parents, like all others, must advocate for education changes, be willing to engage alternate education routes, educate themselves on what is and is not taking place in our public schools, and do what is best for their own children as unique individuals.

Our public education system now legally requires teachers to educate every pupil from standardized instructional methods and curriculum. We are currently providing American youth with homogenized lesson plans with mandated timelines and test-taking deadlines. Our students are *not* simply members of a massive national student body but also individuals uniquely designed for a purposeful life by our Creator. Squelching teacher and student individualism will certainly impact our future vitality and innovation as a nation. When we take notice and take action, a standardized education might be defined as preparing *all* our nation's youth (including those students who are accelerated learners) with thorough solid knowledge in core subjects at challenging levels. We *can* better ensure all students have access to the best opportunities and necessary programs to advance their knowledge and meet their needs at appropriate levels. Our national future—our true national treasures—should never be labeled ineligible to pursue their potentials as our child was. Each child is a shining star, and each is deserving his or her appropriate taxpayer-funded education under our existing national guarantee.

Parental Involvement

Parents generally believe they know their children better than anyone else—and they usually do! They generally take responsibility for getting their children's needs met when it comes to shelter, clothing, food, religious instruction, and recreation activities. When it comes to their children's academic needs, however, too many parents disconnect as soon as they drop their children at the bus stop or on the school grounds. I have seen passivity (taking the attitude that educators know best or know all) used as positioning for blaming instructors later—when parents didn't like the results their children obtained. While some parents are completely uninvolved with their children's educations and have submissively surrendered their children's learning to the system currently in place, other parents attempt to work with their local public schools to resolve issues and contribute to making public education better at their local level. Many parents have been consistent unpaid volunteers trying to pick up the slack where budget cuts have left a trail of cancelled programs and lost learning opportunities. Their counterparts (lesser-involved parents) often blamed their school district officials, teachers (a lack of individual attention), or faulty textbooks. Many parents I have spoken with have expressed that current standards, curriculum choices, or teaching methods simply do not work for their children's individual requirements. Often concerned parents have been met with authoritative resistance and don't know what they can do about it. Parents and students alike are often annoyed, having been thwarted by policies and frustrated by professional educators. Some parents have reached such high frustration levels with the inability to attain academic results that they have thrown in the public education towel! A growing trend to combating our nation's broken public education and government bureaucracy controlling our children's learning is homeschooling. On September 3, 2013, president of the Home School Legal Defense Association, J. Michael Smith, wrote,

> The U.S. Department of Education's National Center for Education Statistics (NCES) released an eagerly awaited report on the number of homeschool students in the U.S. The report showed that the number of homeschool students has grown by almost 300,000 since the last report in 2007. The new report concludes that approximately 1,770,000 students are homeschooled in the United States—3.4% of the school-age population. (Smith 2013)

Granted, 3.4 percent is a very small number of the total of our nation's schoolchildren. Still, homeschooling is not likely to slow in growth while public education continues to slide down the slippery slope. There are many opinions regarding homeschooling, but we cannot deny that this consistently growing public education alternative is representative of parental dissatisfaction with government's public educational decisions. *Forbes* contributor Bill Flax explains,

> The God-fearing, flag-waiving, gun-toting homeschool crowd embodies the American spirit of mutual

> self-reliance.... Their support networks blossom sans
> the state's sanction. (Flax 2013)

It would be a blanket generalization to presume that *all* homeschooling families are religious, patriotic, and armed. However, the point is made that self-reliance has provided a better education for growing numbers of youth where public education has failed. Many educators and proponents of public school have tried to downgrade the homeschooling trend. Homeschooling as an alternative has often been on the receiving end of negative connotations. Some homeschooling families have feared the day law enforcement or Department of Education officials would arrive at their door, claiming their child was truant from compulsory education or to take an inventory of their enrolled pupils, survey their homeschool curriculum, and analyze their home classrooms. I have heard some proponents of traditional education (educators too) remark that parents who homeschool are just lazy and taking the easy way out by deviating from the public school norm. The truth is "The homeschool community reflects a cross-section of Americans; the children of truck drivers and lawyers, whites and blacks, rich and poor, Christians and unbelievers" (Flax 2013). Parents who choose to homeschool are reflective of our nation's citizens: the majorities are honest, resourceful and hardworking. These parents have taken personal responsibility to provide a level of education to their youngsters that they believe is unobtainable in public schools.

Many parents of public school students do rely too much on educators to determine the course and speed of their child's education plan. Most educators I have dealt with hold the opinion that all parents should be a considerably more self-reliant and proactive with their children's education. At the same time, some teachers do everything they can to discourage parental interference or distraction in their classrooms. Sadly, our public schools are becoming more like fortresses to prevent *true* gun-toting deviants from harming our children. Parents are not immune to areas where improvement on their parts might take place. Greater parental contribution in equipping students with good manners would be welcomed on every playground and in every classroom. Teachers must have atmospheres where students are well behaved, eager to learn, and able to absorb learning challenges given to them. The old saying that "charity begins at home" could be revitalized to say "education begins at home," and it begins with well-mannered, respectful children well before they enter their teachers' classrooms. Parents who rely solely on the public education system to tell them their children's educational needs will be disappointed. Parents who pay attention to what keeps their children challenged, intrigued, and yearning to grab greater knowledge will be able to work with teachers for greater student learning achievements. Supplying learning challenges at home, and supporting what our children studied at their schools, encouraged our children to complete their educations and to discover more about the directions they wanted to pursue. I think many parents could do a far better job being involved in their children's homework, school experiences, and educational successes. I believe that parents *and* their children both need to put down the joy stick controllers to the video games! By no means am I endorsing the premise that some educators hold, "enrichment is solely the parents' responsibility" but rather that education should come in many ways and from many experiences. Both home and school environments should be educationally enriching arenas. Our public schools do not hold a monopoly on avenues to learning, and teachers and school staff members do not exist to parent any family's "blessings." Public education is not a free childcare service, and teachers are not nannies—though I have seen many parents using public schools for these reasons. When did it become acceptable for so many parents to abdicate their responsibilities to tend to their children's wonderful minds as well as their physical and emotional needs? Instructors who are forced to teach children how to behave in classrooms and on school campuses lose valuable time to teach reading, math, and language arts to their entire classes of students.

As for educators, I have experienced too many who disregarded my own opinions and discouraged my involvement in my children's formal educations, so I empathize with other parents who face similar attitudes. Often teachers stood on their own esteemed degrees in education, criticizing my parental presence, inquiries, or suggestions concerning my children and their academic performances. Nearly all were against radical acceleration as our education path for Sara. A former practice we should all seek to remember, and restore to our society, is the benefit to every student's life when both parents and professional teachers display mutual respect rather than "a haughty spirit" (Proverbs 16:18 NASB). Instructors need an atmosphere in which to teach—something that has been all but vanquished from modern classrooms. Parents are usually intelligent beings who also impart significant learning experiences and deserve their due respect. The atmosphere in which students can learn has become more difficult for teachers to control. In my opinion, to maximize learning success, students need the opportunity to absorb subject material for the subject mastery (not for the methodology that they will be tested on to meet government regulations) as well as involved parents, less stressed-out teachers (who can retain passion for their profession), and environments where classmates are behaved rather than disruptive.

Legislation and Standardized Testing

All children are unique individuals. As such, not all children perform at the same level, in the same time frame, or learn in the same way. The answer to what specifically *is* an appropriate public education is: the one that meets the student's needs! It stands to reason that *all* our nation's children should have equal access to programs in education that assist them toward success. No doubt departments of education will continue to develop new programs, and politicians will bring more legislation. Many special needs programs currently *are* in place. The effectiveness of those programs, and seeming lack of benefits from some existing legislation are issues to resolve. Some education decisions have *not* achieved optimal (or measurable) success preparing students for their future and ours. The National Center for Education Statistics has reported our high school students' consistent performances between 2000 and 2012. The statistics compiled by PISA are disturbing.

The Program for International Student Assessment (PISA) is an international assessment that measures 15-year-old students' reading, mathematics, and science literacy. PISA also includes measures of general or cross-curricular competencies, such as problem solving. PISA emphasizes functional skills that students have acquired as they near the end of compulsory schooling. (U. D. Education n.d.)

US students have placed well below the top, sliding down and bouncing up only a few points over the five testing years between 2000 and 2012. US students are sitting at thirty-sixth for math, thirty-eighth for science, and forty-second in reading when compared to the same age high school students of sixty-four other countries listed. Latest PISA examinations place Shanghai, Hong Kong, and Singapore in the top three placings. In every subject area, our students' 2012 scores fell from the previous testing results of 2009, while Shanghai's, Hong Kong's, and Singapore's students' scores all increased. After all our focus on testing, teaching the material on the tests, standardized instruction, and legislated mandates for proving pupil improvement by testing, our students' scores still fell! This is the type of bright beacon illuminating public education and legislated mandates that concerns parents and sends them seeking alternate education routes. What happened to the good old basics in education that previous generations of amazing men and women (now successful in their endeavors) had received? There are physicians, attorneys, and corporate leaders who were public school educated. There are hardworking laborers and dedicated parents who attended public schools as well. To quote my own grandmother, "Have we thrown the baby out with the bathwater?" Supporting excellent teachers, who are permitted to instill thorough knowledge until students master subjects completely, is a good idea to slow our students from continuing down the slippery slope of declining knowledge. If we want our students to be globally competitive in the future, we're going to have to come together nationally with something better than our same failing strategies.

Rising crime rates and teenage pregnancies have been correlated to our nation's public school problems. Our declining educational dollars and the resulting cancelled program opportunities for our youth are often blamed. Certainly problems with education are not the sole cause of these and other issues. A lack of employment opportunities, economic strife, and family dynamics are also in play. However, budget cuts to education have no doubt created a trickledown effect of apathy and set or assist the feet of some young people on a downward-spiraling path. What boggles the minds of many including myself is how, with all our understanding of the importance of knowledge, we have left our brightest future behind in a public education system that isn't working. American children are blessed to have the right to a free and appropriate education (FAPE) and with it the responsibility to study hard, learn much, and do something with the gift the taxpayers have provided to them. Education paid by the taxpayers is a tremendous provision for American youth. However, it poses equally tremendous challenges. What specifically is an appropriate public-funded education? Our national goal is providing nondiscriminatory and quality learning experiences for all. Our nationally approved statistics agency[12] reports we have raised our high-school graduation rates, while simultaneously our high-school-student test scores have lowered or flatlined. Are we providing our young adults a quality learning experience? Is the No Child Left Behind Act of 2001 truly accomplishing its intent?

> To close the achievement gap with accountability, flexibility, and choice, so that no child is left behind" and the purpose of which is "to ensure that all children have a fair, equal, and significant opportunity to obtain a high-quality education and reach, at a minimum, proficiency on challenging State academic achievement standards and state academic assessments. (US Department of Education n.d.)

Solving our national education issues isn't as simple as throwing more federal taxpayer dollars at convoluted problems. There are individual priorities within each state and at local district levels. There is the problem solving of what appropriate curriculum is. There is also a problem with the time process that curriculum is distributed (age/grade-based education). There is the responsibility to meet special needs of individual students without bias or prejudice. Interpretation of policies by individual schools, districts, and states at times discriminates in determining who should receive assistance in the form of specialized programming and who should not. Not one of these problems will be solved by cutting funding,

---

[12] The National Center for Education Statistics (NCES) is the primary federal entity for collecting and analyzing data related to education.

though government has diverted educational funding to pay debts that our legislators continued to accrue elsewhere. We have reduced funding for educational preparation of the future in order to cover the abundant budget errors our elected officials have produced in the present. Addition or subtraction of dollars will not miraculously fix what is broken with our public education system. It will take more than money. Our current education system provides a one size fits all design. My husband commented, "Each student enters the system, usually in kindergarten around age five, and proceeds though a conveyer belt process and exits the twelfth grade at ages seventeen or eighteen." We are mass producing students with greater government hovering and lower achievements. Students, having received virtually identical subject instructions, attained passing marks meeting minimum requirements, and reached age and grade levels, are issued high school diplomas. We have a standardized education system! Sadly, regardless of individual abilities the conveyer moves forward at the same pace for all. Some students would have benefited and learned more with more time. Others may have benefited being allowed to move along faster. Legal mandates on teachers have caused education to meet government timelines with specific requirements and teach to test materials. Conveying deeper subject information to children until they had thoroughly learned it—whether at grade level or ability level—may have been the goal at one time, but it has been bogged down in legalities that have focused on our conveyer belt running systematically.

Our nation's students need to be prepared with the ability to take on societal issues because they can truly comprehend and reason logical methods to solve challenges. These young people will be the problem solvers of our future and should receive not an adequate education but a great one! Our students should be permitted the thrill of gaining subject knowledge even if it is not on a standardized test. The taxpaying citizens financially support public education, but it is the elected officials in politics, those appointed to various positions within the Department of Education, and local school board officials that possess the authority to sway and impact the thoughts and beliefs taught to fresh, young minds. A student may have received a diploma at the end of the K–12 compulsory grades, but many taxpayers do not know what students are being taught or what they *haven't* learned. What we do know is that students passed the *minimum* required subject *area* on a required standardized test. Young Americans will eventually attain adulthood and, as adults in our society, possess the right vote. Unless as a nation we are comfortable with the attributes of a current teen idol as our future president, we should be deeply alarmed by the continued decline of our national education in properly preparing our future voters to make wise choices when electing leadership. Some may believe that interactions between foreign governments' leaderships and American celebrities are a good thing. Frankly, it scares me to think foreign policy decisions may one day be made by a president elected on popularity because of his or her win/loss record as a former professional athlete or having been a celebrity icon. The ability to invoke beneficial future legislation must come from properly educating our youth while we have opportunity to do so. We must convey to them the importance of reasoning and researching *all* the issues they will face (many issues will not be on a standardized test). Students should be following current events, with significant knowledge of past ones, in order to comprehend the depth of *real* issues as expertly as they navigate computer video games. America's problematic educational system will likely continue until the majority of voters invoke changes to it. Addressing education problems begins by discussing issues then progresses into problem solving. Our legislators and departments of education appear to have their work behind, beside, and ahead of them while solutions remain far off. Perhaps a *balance* should be sought: some autonomy for teachers (who best can ascertain the learning style and needs of their own local pupils); ensuring our national education bar is challenging (and attainable) by allowing teachers to determine *when* their pupils are test ready (having had full exposure to material); focusing on "core" (basic) subject areas at length; supplying nondiscriminatory federal funding of "special needs' programs for all; getting the focus back to *ability levels* and off of age/grade-based obsessions; and reducing class sizes nationally. These might be wise choices. We need to improve our public education for *all* students. We need legislators who, without repressing student and teacher individuality, will commit to meet needs in ways that will work. If we continue the direction we are headed I am concerned we will arrive at permanently homogenized school system. Merriam-Webster gave this example for homogenize. "The new curriculum is an attempt to *homogenize* education throughout the county." (Merriam-Webster n.d.) Understanding what is required, prohibited, and what remains needed by all students in our current

187

education system allows us to ascertain how to improve our nation's preparation of future generations. We can only yield the best educated and well-prepared future leaders and voters if we invest in them—all of them! Perhaps a return to education basics where instructors teach subject matters thoroughly until students have mastered concepts is indeed a better plan. Perhaps teachers with time to answer student inquiries is more conducive to learning. Perhaps if relieved from government demands that they synchronize their lesson times and teaching methods "to the tests" that politicians have legislated them to follow, teachers would remain in their professions and our students would be well rounded and proficient in knowledge. When I consider the many issues with public education, I am convinced that removing prayer from our public schools was not the issue legislators needed to concern themselves with. At this late education hour, getting prayer back into public education would certainly be a place to begin the reversal of the downward spiral that has resulted from decades of bureaucratic micromanagement.

Funding a Program for the Gifted

Some of Sara's teachers, tasked with requirements to ensure their failing students hit the mark, often let go of instructing her since she was surpassing the mark at extremely high levels. Disengaged students like Sara often go quietly off to an isolation corner. Some accelerated children will be satisfied working independently until social time at lunch. Others may be greatly disappointed. We witnessed our child developing a lackluster attitude toward school in a public system without appropriate education accommodations in place. At some point, it is time to stop blaming and act upon the needs of our individual students—especially if no contracts, no interventions, and no adequate higher challenges are available. If ability level challenges are going to be available to all our students, and not exempt our young gifted, then parents like me must be proactive advocates for them. Our education system is choking our nation's bright future with continued age/grade focus. Our gifted pupils represent a small fraction of our nation's students and our world's citizens. Intellectually bright individuals are dispersed nationally and globally. As a nation, we have continued to deny they are a special-needs group deserving federal funding and access to their appropriate instruction opportunities. Federal funding should be made available to meet the special needs of gifted— needs that have repeatedly been defined by consistent research and experts. Appropriate opportunities should be available even if a school's exceptionally gifted population totals one student. We have a moral, if not a legal, responsibility in America to provide for the special needs of all our students. If we are going to state that *all* the children in the United States are entitled to FAPE and that each must attend twelve years of compulsory education, then nationally we should provide for the diagnosed special needs of student population groups as we have become aware. The arbitrary determination allowed by self-governing school districts in California creates great disparity. A system where individual school administrators arbitrarily determine with absolute authority what shall be deemed "appropriate" and who consider the needs of the gifted a mere "optional enrichment" is unacceptable. Providing so called *enrichment* to gifted students at the whim of each administrator is absurd! How do we justify meeting the special needs of ESL learners, RSP students, provide IEP's for all students with special needs due to recognized "disability," and put into place necessary "504 plans" while simultaneously denying funding of a single federal program recognizing the special-needs requirements of the nation's gifted population? Specialists with PhDs in education and psychology, esteemed experts in giftedness, and multitudes of research have repeatedly reached the same conclusions. Due to the very nature of their exceptional minds, gifted students do indeed have special needs in education. There are many more "Saras" in need of an advocate and desperately seeking ability level opportunities in their educations. This is a discrimination that our national and state government officials should be embarrassed to have called to their attention. We have a population with the capacity to serve humanity is great ways, make new discoveries in difficult areas, and use God-given abilities at maximum potential. Age/grade education focus is holding students back from their capable learning opportunities and developmentally delaying their potential to provide great returns both nationally and globally. Perhaps, when voters take to the polls and more legislators are made aware of students like Sara, positive change will occur. Other students with driven desires to learn at accelerated speeds exist. Their own gifted abilities too need nurturing. Many may be capable of following the precedents in determined education that Sara has set (they too will require funding). Funding gifted education is not solely for the gifted individual but for society in general.

Epilogue

Our journey to secure Sara's appropriate education has been very educational for me! Sara's intelligence quotient has been *a number* that was required to open doors of opportunity. However, many people have jumped to "what's your number" as though it is indicative of certain greatness. There are many IQ assessments, and each has its own scoring matrix. The "number" (that may indicate the same abilities as another IQ assessment with a lower score) should not be perceived as a guarantee of success. Learning outcomes are best when focus is on students achieving at their levels of individual ability and at their own pace. It is not age, grade level, or IQ numbers where our public education needs ridged focus. Learning environments should encourage all students to work at their current ability levels while accepting that students paces to master core subjects thoroughly will be uniquely their own. This is one area in which our public education system could adjust its strategy. Our current national education strategy has not been successful in mass producing identical "products" on its standardized schedule very well! Our students are individual learners with individual gifts and fabulous attributes. Not all will do well in our current traditional pathway of public education. Most patriots want our nation's students to be well educated. Let's help each attain thorough instruction. Expanding our students' learning with exposure to areas not on standardized tests, and ensuring long-term retention of material through subject mastery would benefit them. Some will learn concepts and master subjects faster, and some will be slower, because we all have uniquely created areas of potential—whatever our "number" may be. All our current and previous legislation mandating standardized testing and curriculum has not increased our students' abilities to compete globally. Foreign students who are the age/grade peers of our national student body are consistently better prepared. I do not believe copying the educational systems from another culture is the answer (and it has previously been tried). Perhaps it would be prudent to take a look at our own sociologic and cultural changes from previous generations and readjust our current strategies for better future outcomes.

It is my prayer that you have found this reflection of our journey informative and encouraging. I also pray other parents who have been perceived as rebels (like myself) have found it validating. More importantly, my prayers are for other struggling students to be encouraged by the joy Sara has now found. I pray that all readers will be motivated to investigate ballot measures thoroughly and exercise their rights to vote. Voters can effect change for the betterment of our educational system. "But select capable men from all the people—men who fear God, trustworthy men who hate dishonest gain—and appoint them as officials over thousands, hundreds, fifties and tens" (Exodus 18:21 NIV). Finally, I pray that God continues to bless all children—and their horses! I am grateful for the many who have prayed and continue to pray for my entire family. I am thankful to God who has been exceedingly gracious and generous to me.

To protect her privacy and allow her to grow up in as normal an American childhood as possible, we have always allowed Sara to tell us the level of publicity she has been ready to handle. My motivation with the telling of Sara's educational journey now has been to inform other students, parents, educators, and legislators why some students *do* in fact require alternative paths to reach an end result of successful education. Of course, *now* it is also our hope to generate a volume of sales of this self-published book that will assist in funding Sara's current and continuing education—as extremely few scholarship opportunities exist for which she meets age/grade application requirements.

As a fifteen-year-old at Mary Baldwin College, Sara Hise made the dean's list both semesters. She carried a load of fourteen fall semester and fifteen spring semester upper-division units. If you wish to assist Sara in limiting her student debt as she continues to pursue her higher education with her baccalaureate and master's degrees, donations are accepted (view additional information) at:

www.youcaring.com/helpsara

Like her at **Sara's Saga** on Facebook (view some of her commendations) at:

https://www.facebook.com/helpsarahise
Congratulations to all alumnae of MBC
PEG and Early College Academy!
We look forward to the day Sara joins
you in alumnae status.

Photo Credit: Jenny Hazlewood

Bibliography

2015. *Autism Society.* Accessed June 14, 2015. http://www.autism-society.org/what-is/symptoms/.

n.d. *California Department of Education.* Accessed Jan 1, 2015. http://www.cde.ca.gov/ci/gs/hs/hsgrmin.asp.

Cloud, John. 2007. "Are We Failing Our Geniuses." *Time Magazine.* August 16. Accessed April 16, 2013. http://content.time.com/time/magazine/article/0,9171,1653653,00.html.

Cushman, Karen. 1996. *The Ballad of Lucy Whipple.* New York, New York: Houghton Mifflin. Accessed June 2008.

Education, California Department of. n.d. "Law & Regulations - Gifted & Talented Education." *California Department of Education.* Accessed March 6, 2013. http://www.cde.ca.gov/sp/gt/lw/index.asp?print=yes.

Education, US Department of. n.d. *Institute of Sciences, Program for International Student Assessment.* Accessed Dec. 30, 2014. http://nces.ed.gov/surveys/pisa/pisa2012/pisa2012highlights_6a.asp.

Flax, Bill. 2013. "Want To Tell The State To Stick It? Homeschool Your Kids." *Forbes.* January 22. Accessed November 23, 2013. http://www.forbes.com/sites/billflax/2013/01/22/want-to-tell-the-state-to-stick-it-homeschool-your-kids/.

Foner, Eric. 2009. *Give Me Liberty! An American History.* Second Seagull Edition. Edited by Lory A. Frenkel. Vols. Two - Second Edition. New York, New York: W. W. Norton & Company, Inc. Accessed 2011.

Hise, Sara. 2008-2014. *Personal Writings of Sara Hise.* Ridgecrest, CA, USA: Sara Hise.

—. 2008. *Sara's Bookworm Reviews*. Accessed November 2013. sarasbookwormreviews.blogspot.com.

Hoffman, E.T.A. 1816. *The Nutcracker and the Mouse King*. Germany.

1996. *Holy Bible - New Living Translation*. Wheaton, Illinois, USA: Tyndale House Publishers, Inc.

Institute, Davidson. n.d. "Davidson Institute for Talent Development." *davidsongifted.org*. Accessed March 6, 2013. http://www.davidsongifted.org/db/Articles_print_id_10363. aspx.

Lobel, Arnold. 1970. *Frog and Toad are Friends*. New York, NY: HarperCollins Publishers Inc.

n.d. *Merriam Webster*. Accessed Jan 1, 2015. http://www.merriam-webster.com/dictionary/homogenize.

1999. *NASB Study Bible (New American Standard Bible)*. Grand Rapids, Michigan, USA, Michigan: Zondervan Publishing House. Accessed 2013.

2008. *National Association For Gifted Children*. Accessed June 14, 2015. http://www.nagc.org/traits-giftedness#sthash.24IClCen. dpufv.

Nye, Joseph S., Jr. 2002. *The Paradox of American Power: Why The World's Only Superpower Can't Go It Alone*. New York, New York: Oxford University Press. Accessed 2011.

Obama, Barack, President of the United States. 2010. "Presidential Award of Outstanding Academic Excellence." Washington, D.C., March 17.

O'Reilly, Bill and Charles Flowers. 2007. *Kids Are Americans Too*. Edited by Hope Innelli. New York, New York: HarperCollins Publishers. Accessed August 2009.

Palmer, David. 2006. *Parents' Guide to IQ Testing and Gifted Education*. Edited by Judith Myers and Carl Minturn. Long Beach, CA: Quality Books. Accessed 2011.

Plowman, Paul D. 1971. "California Mentally Gifted Minor Program: A Brief History." California Department of Education, Sacramento. Accessed March 7, 2013. http://www. eric.ed.gov/ERICWebPortal/search/detailmini.jsp?_nfpb+t ...

Skloot, Rebecca. 2010. *The Immortal Life of Henrietta Lacks.* New York, New York: Crown Publishers. Accessed 2010.

Smith, J. Michael. Esq. 2013. *HSLDA.* September 3. Accessed December 23, 2014. http://www.hslda.org/docs/ news/2013/201309030.asp.

Solomon, Andrew. 2012. *Far From The Tree.* New York, New York: Simon & Schuster, Inc. Accessed May 16, 2013.

Solomon, Andrew. 2012. "Would You Wish This On Your Child?" *New York Times Magazine.* November 4. Accessed April 16, 2013. http://www.nytimes.com/2012/11/04/magazine/how-do-you-raise-a-prodigy.html?_r=0.

1987. *The Amplified Cross Reference Bible.* Grand Rapids, Michigan, USA: Zondervan.

2011. *The Holy Bible, New International Version, NIV.* Grand Rapids, Michigan, USA: Zondervan.

1982. *The Holy Bible, New King James Version.* Birmingham, Alabama, USA: BARDIN & MARSEE PUBLISHING.

Thomas, George and Joseph Crescimbeni. 1966. *Guiding the Gifted Child.* New York, New York: Random House. Accessed April 16, 2013.

n.d. *US Department of Education.* Accessed Jan 2, 2015. http:// www2.ed.gov/policy/elsec/leg/esea02/pg1.html.

Untermeyer, Louis. 2002. *Robert Frost's Poems.* New York, New York: St. Martin's Paperbacks. Accessed May 6, 2013.

Acknowledgments

Esther was advised to speak up, not to keep silent, and to consider that she may have been placed in her specific position for the very help that was required at the time (Esther 4:14 NASB). I am thankful to those who have encouraged me (even admonished me to share our child's education journey) to speak up and to write this testimony. Throughout this process, they have supported me, believing this story is relevant to this point in time and to the needs of students in our current public education system. Some have continually reminded me, "Blessed are those who trust in the Lord" (Jeremiah 17:7 NASB). Others have provided additional encouragements: a well-chosen word, countless cups of coffee, a quiet corner, a needed scripture reference, or technological help where my skills are lacking. To Sara's sister, Emma Wright—your closeness with Sara, and your insightful suggestions, throughout her educational journey have been a blessing to me. I express my appreciation to the following individuals who have encouraged me along this journey: Ann Taylor, Lance Sanchez, Lynn Riddick, Judith Norcross, April McMurtrie, Chautona Havig, Kenny Dutton, Anni Dutton, and Candee Coffee. My special thanks to Sarah Witkowski (Library Tech II), and Karen Spurlock (Library Assistant II), at Cerro Coso Community College for the support given me during countless hours spent in that library researching and preparing this book. I am very appreciative of the professionals in education and in spiritual leadership who read and endorsed this manuscript. I am sincerely grateful to Stephanie Ferguson PhD, and Thomas E. Ward, minister of the gospel, for their support. I am honored to acknowledge those instructors who gave to my child a gladness of heart along with higher-level learning challenges. On numerous occasions, Sara has commented that she will never forget her favorite teachers including: Mr. Charles Humphreys, Mr. Dick Benson, Matthew Jones, PhD, and Christine Swiridoff, PhD. These instructors solidified the joy of knowledge that our daughter has always passionately sought. I am grateful to Mrs. Pam Barnes for the many joyful contributions she has provided to Sara's education. I am also very appreciative for the insights and validation provided to me by David Palmer, PhD, whose expertise on giftedness assisted us in discovering ability-level options for Sara. I am grateful to God for the blessing of my husband, Kevin. Each of our children has received his positive influence and been blessed in many ways by my husband's presence in their lives. Together, we have raised remarkable human beings who were entrusted to us by God.

About Tamara Hise

Photo Credit: Jenny Hazlewood

A graduate of Biola University, the author obtained her bachelor of science degree in organizational leadership with high honors. Tammy pursued career goals in municipal government in Southern California prior to relocating with her husband to his hometown in the Mojave Desert. She and her husband, Kevin, have raised five unique children and are embracing their empty-nest adventures. Previously awarded membership in Iota Alpha Chapter of Alpha Sigma Lambda, Tammy remains active and true to "first in scholarship and leadership" by tutoring struggling students. She actively participates in community projects, advocates for civic matters and supports various special needs groups.

Tammy is a longtime member in good standing of Sisters On The Fly and a previous member of California Gymkhana Association—State; CGA, District 23 "Thundering Hooves" and of CGA, District 35 "Los Vaqueros." She is active in her church and her church community.

The author is available for speaking engagements and may be contacted through her author's webpage at WestBow Press.

Printed in the United States
By Bookmasters